Loving Natalee

Loving Natalee

A Mother's Testament of Hope and Faith

Beth Holloway
with Sunny Tillman

HarperOne
An Imprint of HarperCollinsPublishers

HarperOne

Back panel photographs are courtesy of the photographers: Natalee on the motorcycle by Hunter Whitlock; Natalee in cheerleading outfit by Doug Cottis; Natalee's graduation by George "Jug" Twitty; Natalee with her family by Tom Warriner; and Beth Holloway at a chapel in Aruba by Sunny Tillman.

Most photographs in the insert section of this book are from the personal collection of Beth Holloway and used with her permission. Photographs on pages 1, 11, 12, 13 (center and bottom), 14 (except of Beth sitting and reading, which comes from her personal collection), and 15 (top) are reprinted with permission of AP Images. Photographs on page 8 (bottom, left) is reprinted by permission of Brad Dale; and (top, right) is reprinted by permission of Dee Moore. The photograph on the last page of the insert section, of Beth reading Natalee's journal, is reprinted by permission of photographer Randal Crow, www.randalcrow.com.

HarperCollins books may be purchased for educational, business, or sales promotional use. For information please write: Special Markets Department, HarperCollins Publishers Inc., 10 East 53rd Street, New York, NY 10022.

HarperCollins Web site: http://www.harpercollins.com
HarperCollins®, ⛏®, and HarperOne™ are
trademarks of HarperCollins Publishers

FIRST EDITION
Designed by Joseph Rutt

Library of Congress Cataloging-in-Publication Data is available.

ISBN: 978-0-06-145227-7
ISBN 10: 0-06-145227-0

07 08 09 10 11 RRD(H) 10 9 8 7 6 5 4 3 2 1

Dedicated to my mother, Ann Reynolds,
and to my father, the late Paul Reynolds,
who nurtured me in faith and taught me to be strong.

Life
by Natalee Holloway

Life is a hard journey that we all take.
Unfortunately, it's not equipped with any brakes.

The probability of being perfect is extremely slim.
Indeed, we all have our odds and ends.

Every now and then you are told a lie.
Before you know it ten years have gone by.

Positive thoughts come in by the day.
Negative people take them away.

Time multiplies our days to years.
Every now and then we shed a tear.

In life, love should be the base.
We must cherish every face.

Contents

Contents

Author's Note

The following account comes from my memory, conversations, and notes I kept of the events that took place surrounding the disappearance of my daughter, Natalee Holloway. I have tried to relate to the best of my recollection what took place during this crisis. Quotation marks are used in the book for the purposes of readability, not necessarily to indicate that the words in quotes are exact.

Acknowledgments

The first person who suggested I write a book about Natalee's disappearance was Jamie Skeeters, the polygraph expert sent to the island by Dr. Phil McGraw. Jamie died in January 2007. He was on the phone with his wife during a connecting flight when he suffered a massive heart attack. The plane was still on the tarmac when Jamie died in his seat. Jamie worked very, very hard on Natalee's case and we all miss him very much. When I got to a place in my life that I felt I was ready to tell what happened surrounding my daughter's disappearance, I was so pleased when senior editor Maureen O'Brien called from Harper-Collins to say they wanted to publish this book. I'm grateful to everyone at HarperCollins and HarperOne for this opportunity. I just wish Jamie were here to see that Natalee's story has finally been told.

Throughout this account I've tried to recognize the individuals, companies, and organizations that have played a significant role in helping our family pursue justice for Natalee, and want to again thank all of them for their support. In addition, I want to especially thank Governor and Mrs. Bob Riley and all the Alabama representatives who stood behind us; the FBI; the media; Heather and Phillip McWane; Richard Rogers; the National Sheriff's Association and the National Association of School Resource Officers for their endorsements of the Safe Travels campaign; Baker Crow; the LeMay family; Ashley Cockrell for the *Natalee Run*; High Noon Film and Interactive, LLC; Auburn University; Florida State University's Underwater Crime Scene Investigation Unit; Texas Equu-Search; John Q. Kelly; Dr. Phil McGraw; Fred Golba; Jossy Mansur; and the Aruban citizens who gave their support.

Also, special thanks go to Red at Scared Monkeys, and to all the kind helpful bloggers who have supported our family, from Blogs for Natalee to Truth for Natalee, and all the others. You have truly been a source of great support as well as providing important and useful information.

Without Natalee's friends, my friends, the good people of Mountain Brook, and everyone else who reached out, we would not have been able to achieve what we have on this journey. We didn't get Natalee back, but everyone gave it his or her very best. And we could not have asked for more than that. I want to thank everyone involved from the bottom of my heart. God bless you all.

Preface

I'm the parent who got the dreaded call. The parent no one wants to be. The one whose phone rang out of the blue in the middle of the day, and the voice on the other end said, "Your daughter is missing." I'm that desperate mother on TV holding up pictures of her missing child, pleading for help, describing the details surrounding an unthinkable crime. My daughter is Natalee Holloway. She disappeared in Aruba on the last night of her senior-high graduation trip in 2005 and hasn't been seen since. I never imagined that I would be "that parent," living an endless nightmare in front of the whole world. But I was, and I still am, because I will always search for her. I will forever be Natalee's mom.

Two questions are most often asked of me since Natalee's disappearance. One is, "How do you keep going on this journey to find her?" My answer is always, "Hope." At one time or another we've all experienced hope. That inexplicable empowerment that enables us to move successfully from challenge to resolution with courage. The guarantee that there's light at the end of whatever tunnel we're trying to find our way through. It's more than just a feeling. More than wishful thinking, I believe hope is the almost tangible reaction to one's faith. But let me tell you, it's easy to lose when you're faced with bitter tragedy. It's easy to give in to pain and let go of all hope. I learned this first-hand when Natalee disappeared. I've learned a lot of things about hope since then.

Bridging beliefs from Judaism to Catholicism, from Protestantism to Mormonism, from Islam to Buddhism and everything in between, hope is a religious message common to all faiths. The universal message that better times are ahead is nourishment for the soul, just as food is nourishment for the body. Hope comes in many different forms, and each one of us reaches for the one that will satisfy our hunger. For me it means reaching for the next sign of hope, and the next, and the next that will lead me to what happened to Natalee. I find hope, it fades, and then I grow hungry for it again. One sign of hope doesn't sustain us, as I learned. We have to keep reaching for it. And that's the very definition of resilience.

Hope presented itself to me in the most likely as well as the most unlikely places. I found it first in God, centered on a firm foundation of faith established by my parents in my childhood in the Methodist Church. I also found hope in the unwavering support from our hometown community and in the volunteers who came from the United States and other countries to help me search for Natalee. I found it in every anonymous tip that she had been seen alive. It was there in thousands of letters and cards with prayers and encouraging words from caring people all around the world. The best way to describe it is that hope came as surges of energy. Big, bright, vibrant waves of energy that washed across my soul the same way the ocean tide comes to shore and smoothes out the sand. Then it went away, ebbed, like the tide. But it always came back. And that's the most important realization in this tragic experience—that no matter what, just as sure as the tide rolls in, *hope always comes.*

I've learned very important life lessons about survival in the face of tragedy since Natalee disappeared. First, hope is always obtainable, but sometimes we overlook it and fail to embrace it. There have been many times on this long and painful journey that I forgot to recognize the signs and began to lose hope. But I found out that all I had to do was reach for it, let it in, consume it. What a gift we have before us. The second important lesson is that faith knows no boundaries. It doesn't matter what your religious preference is when it comes to reaching out to people in need. It doesn't matter which church or temple you attend when it comes to prayer. What matters is that you express this love. That you share this *hope.* That you give comfort by asking God to bring peace to someone. People from all walks of faith have done this for me, and it has saved my life.

Without hope we are hungry. And on a very deep level, desperate. But no one has to be. What's so amazing is that we can feed each other. We can help each other. We have the power to give resilience to others who are fading. We can nourish each other's spirits and save one another from defeat and despair. Every one of us possesses this power to "love thy neighbor," and we need to use it every chance we get. People did this for me. They constantly gave me signs of hope. I would exhaust each one and look for the next one. And it always came.

Natalee always had friends of many different faiths. Some of her friends in Birmingham attend Temple Emanu-El. In a sermon delivered to his congregation to address Natalee's disappearance, Rabbi Jonathan Miller, who I think is a very wise man in our community, defined hope, saying: "We have learned that when things become the darkest, that is when we are called upon to envision the light. We have learned that when everything has gone wrong, that is when we have to believe that things can be made right again. That is the message of hope. We must never abandon hope. We must never let darkness extinguish the light. We must remain hopeful." Rabbi Miller is absolutely right about that.

The second question people, especially reporters, ask me so often is, "How do you feel?" I've avoided the answer to that one until now. Because Natalee's story was the number one reported news event for 2005 and was still in the top ten for 2006, it made headlines all over the world. And still does. Many, many people heard about our crisis and poured out their prayers for my family and me. If I had described in all those media interviews what I was really going through, these good people might have thrown up their hands and stopped praying. And that's the last thing we needed. I was afraid if I revealed the true anguish and despair we were experiencing and broke down in front of the cameras for all the world to see, those who were praying for us would simply give up, decide it was a hopeless cause. I had received so much sympathy and empathy and was so grateful for it that I didn't want to let anyone down. I thought it best to keep my feelings and the behind-the-scenes situation private and just try to stand strong.

It wasn't easy for me to be on the receiving end of all this giving. As a schoolteacher of special-needs children for more than twenty-two years, I was always the one who nurtured and gave to others. I was always the one who provided the guidance, comfort, and support. As a single mother, I was always independent, used to taking care of my children and having the answers for everything. But when I lost my child, I was thrown to the other side of that equation. Instead of giving help, I had to receive it. That has made me deeply humble. Thankfully, what I received were the two things I needed the most to survive this crisis: hope and prayers. These gifts are the evidence of faith. And with hope, prayer, and faith a human being can endure almost anything. I'm proof of that.

A lot of healing has taken place since my daughter disappeared. I have waited to tell this story until I felt good about where I am now, instead of revealing where I was then. I'm strong enough now to face the sorrow on my own without having to rely on others. It's time to share everything, from the depths of suffering to the heights of spiritual renewal, so that others may learn and benefit from this experience. I'm finally ready to tell what happened in the summer of 2005.

But this is not an account of the investigation into Natalee's disappearance. Anyone can access that information on the Internet and through the media. This is the inside story of what occurred during the most horrific and tragic event any family could ever imagine. It has to be told because I represent every parent, and Natalee represents every young adult. No one else should ever live this nightmare. If the words that follow will help another parent, child, young adult, or traveler of any age stay safer, then it will have been well worth the writing of this book. That's why it's important for me to tell you what happened and how it happened, how I felt and how I reacted all along this tragic journey. And to finally answer the questions I've been asked a thousand times. So this is my account, the way I experienced it, the way I remember it.

Following is the story no one should have to tell about the nightmare no one wants to live told by the parent no one wants to be. But what happened to Natalee Holloway and the circumstances following her disappearance on the last night of her senior-high trip to Aruba is the story that everyone needs to hear.

In Natalee's Room

It's early morning, and the house is quiet. I'm still lying in bed, eyes closed. I don't want to open them, because when I do, I'll have to face the day I've dreaded the most for the past twenty months. Today I have to pack up Natalee's things for the last time. Today I will have to say the final good-bye. And I'm not ready.

Eyes still closed, I hear an occasional car pass in front of the house. Another one stops across the street, and I hear the car door open, letting music and cheerful muffled voices escape for a moment. Then close again. The stillness in the house is interrupted by the harmonious tapping of little paws as Macy the dog and Carl the cat move across the hardwood floors. Stopping for a moment. Then tapping again. The cold morning brings the sounds of life's activities as people step into another day of their routines. Maybe if I don't open my eyes this day will just pass, and I won't have to face what I have to do. The painful inevitable chore that has been looming over me since my beautiful daughter, Natalee, disappeared on the last night of her senior high school trip to Aruba. The day has come to take her room apart and box it up. I have to go through her belongings, which have remained untouched since she left home on May 26, 2005. The movers will be here day after tomorrow.

Nothing from my life before Natalee disappeared in Aruba has remained intact. Not my career. Not my home. Not my marriage. My husband, Jug, and I are divorcing after six years. My son, Natalee's younger brother, Matt, and I are moving in two days. I have a lot to do. I manage to swing my legs off the bed and sit up. Reluctantly, I open my eyes and sit on the edge for a few moments. I feel like concrete. Heavy. Very heavy. Finally I stand up and slowly walk a half dozen steps or so down the short hall and turn right at Natalee's bedroom doorway.

The morning light shines in through the wall-length windows at the far side of the room illuminating all her neatly organized things. It used to be in disarray most of the time. But today everything in here is in order. It's cheerful and sad at the same time. Light purple—her favorite—and delicate greens. A crisp white bedspread. Pillows with special sayings about friends and love and life. In the corner a purple-painted curio cabinet with four shelves holds all of her treasures. Her collection of *Wizard of Oz* memorabilia is prominently displayed in the tall narrow cabinet. To my right I see her white high-school graduation robe hanging on the outside of the closet door, the honors cords still around the neck. Inside this closet are two beautiful sundresses we bought for her to take to college, the tags still on them. And behind those is the little black dress she wore to her proms, both junior and senior. Photos of friends and certificates of her many achievements are visible everywhere. A bulletin board over her daybed is covered with reminders of meetings and events and parties coming up. She had big plans.

It's an average, modest bedroom. It was just right for Natalee, and she loved it in here. It was her place to work and her place of solace. It's where she giggled with friends and studied for tests. It's where she dressed for the prom. Where she donned her graduation robe. Where she packed for her trip to Aruba. It's Natalee's own space, and everything in it represents her. She was a hardworking young lady, full of life. Smart, gutsy, determined, and very dependable. She had always been that way.

NATALEE AND HER YOUNGER BROTHER, Matt, were born in Memphis, Tennessee, where my first husband, Dave, and I had moved after college. Natalee was three years old and Matt was one when we left Memphis and moved the family to Clinton, Mississippi. Dave and I divorced shortly thereafter. It was a long arduous battle, but I was finally awarded sole custody of both children.

The three of us were tight-knit. Matt and Natalee were very protective of their mother. One night when they were elementary-school age I was going to go out for dinner. I discovered my escort sitting on my front porch with his head buried in his hands. I looked up to see my two children pounding his car with Matt's *metal cleats*. I was so embarrassed! And very surprised— shocked—that they would do such a thing. They apparently didn't want anybody at their mama's house. They were punished accordingly, and I had to repair his paint job. I don't remember that guy ever coming back. The story must have gotten around, because I dated rather infrequently in the years that followed.

After I had been divorced from the children's father for about seven years, I met George "Jug" Twitty while he was on business in Mississippi. We dated for about three years before marrying in 2000. Matt and Natalee absolutely loved his two older children, Megan and George, and looked forward to moving to the lovely bedroom community of Mountain Brook in Birmingham, Alabama, to join their new family and start their new life. Mountain Brook is about as stark a contrast to where I grew up as one could imagine. Back in Pine Bluff, Arkansas, I was the only white girl in my ninth-grade study hall, and one of about three in my history class. Many of my friends were black in this small, unassuming town. All my life, including seventeen years teaching in Mississippi and Arkansas, I have lived in culturally and racially diverse communities. So have my children. It never occurred to me that it wasn't like that everywhere, because I simply never thought about it.

Mountain Brook, one of a number of municipalities that comprise the greater Birmingham area, is an affluent, almost all-white community of about 22,000. I learned after only a few visits here that many people think if you live in Mountain Brook, you must be wealthy. Monetarily speaking, it is an upscale community. And there are a handful of individuals who are heirs to construction, insurance, and the great iron and steel fortunes that were made in the early 1900s. Steelmaking and the civil rights movement are the two historic characteristics Birmingham is known for worldwide. A few of these iron and steel heirs are truly wealthy in every sense of the word. But what I found is that the vast majority of Mountain Brook people are hardworking, two-income families just like us, who are good, solid, middle- to upper-middle-class Americans. My children and I were welcomed with open arms when we moved to Mountain Brook. And I was fortunate to get a great job at one of the elementary schools as a speech pathologist in a center for children with special needs. Wonderful friendships were cultivated with my colleagues there. Matt and Natalee made friends fast and fit right in. And the wives of Jug's group of close friends went out of their way to help us settle into our new community. We were off to a good start.

Natalee was entering the eighth grade when we moved to Mountain Brook in Birmingham. It was about this same time that she developed a true love affair with the movie *The Wizard of Oz*. She began to collect any and all memorabilia she could find pertaining to that movie including posters, a piggy bank, a clock, and even a little purse with Dorothy on it. Once she said that if she had to be stuck on an elevator with anyone, she hoped it would be Judy Garland! Natalee would continue adding to her special Oz collection all through high school.

From the time she was three years old, Natalee looked forward to her weekly dancing lessons. She loved to dance and continued working on her talent throughout her childhood. She was prepared to try out for the high-school theatrical dance team in Clinton. They called it a "show choir." When we moved to Birmingham, she set her sights on trying out for the dance team in her new town. This meant she had to learn a few new routines to be ready for the highly competitive Mountain Brook High School "Dorians." She spent her entire eighth-grade year preparing for the ninth-grade tryout. It was hard work, but that was not a new concept for her.

Displaying an innate drive to be her best, Natalee always worked very hard at everything she did. She was an all-around success story: she made friends easily, she made straight A's, she made the National Honor Society. She thrived in Birmingham. When she needed a higher ACT score, she set her sights on a five-point improvement—and achieved it. Natalee took pride in her volunteer work at Habitat for Humanity, the Humane Society, and Hope Lodge. At Hope Lodge she visited regularly with a thirteen-year-old cancer patient. On their last visit Natalee said the little girl had lost all of her pretty hair, and she quietly worried that it really would be their last visit.

Natalee did everything on her own. She was totally independent. I never had to wake her up for school. Never had to get onto her for not doing what she was supposed to do. Except when it came to cleaning up her room. It always looked as if the same tornado that lifted Dorothy's house may have passed right through Natalee's bedroom! Clothes and books and notes were always scattered everywhere—the typical teenager's bedroom.

Natalee applied to colleges and applied for scholarships on her own. She arranged for housing and roommates. From the time she was a little girl, she took charge of her own responsibilities. Because her expectations were so high, she was challenging to rear. Sometimes I feared that she was independent to a fault. I used to joke with her, saying, "Natalee, just ask me some questions, so I can feel like I'm your parent. Humor me." She never needed my help with anything. Except in one area of her life—her clothes.

Thank goodness there was something Natalee needed me for, something she and I could do together. For some reason she appreciated my opinion regarding her attire and trusted me to help her find the things that looked nice on her. She even trusted me enough when I told her that her junior prom dress was so gorgeous on her that she should wear it again for her senior prom. And she did. We went shopping together almost every Saturday morning. She would appear in the kitchen in a fleece jacket with her hair tied up in a ball. Face freshly washed. No makeup. We would head out to spend most of the entire day together. Those were our bonding times. In the car between stores we would talk about important things and silly things, just anything and everything. Those are the memories I cherish most. To this day I still think I may see her across a makeup counter or catch a glimpse of her between the aisles of clothing racks. I still listen for her to call out to me on Saturday mornings to tell me she's ready to go.

———

EACH NIGHT THE GIRLS PRACTICED their Dorian routines until almost midnight. Two nights before the big tryout in ninth grade, Natalee called me, crying. She had dropped into a split and torn her hamstring. It was a bad injury. I immediately called Jug's brother's wife, Marcia, who worked in public relations for the hospital. She helped us find the right therapy for Natalee's injury. For forty-eight hours Natalee worked through excruciating stretches, heat treatments, and other therapies to attempt to make it to the tryouts in time. Natalee was not about to let an injury keep her from her lifelong dream of making the dance team, no matter how bad it hurt. She comes from a long line of strong-willed, tenacious—some may even say stubborn—people.

The source for this personal inner strength and faithful determination can be traced to my parents. They were stern and as fiercely devout as they were demanding. Raised in the Methodist Church, we never missed Sunday school and worship on Sunday. The foundation of my faith that was established in my childhood was nurtured all through my teens as my whole family participated as active church members. Mom and her brother sang in the choir. We attended youth group and other fellowship activities. Then I went on to teach Sunday school and vacation Bible school for many years as I raised my children in the Methodist Church.

I remember my mother always proclaiming, "God is good." She lives by those three words and taught us to as well. My parents were very faithful and reverent people, yet my father in particular was a tough man. He could slice you up with words. When it came to dealing with my brothers, it was physical. He never laid a hand on my mother or me, but he shook an iron fist. There were no crybabies in our house. No quitters allowed. When I became a teenager, my father decided that I should be driving on my own. Way before I turned sixteen that's just what I did. No license. No driver's ed. He was ready for me to drive, and that was that. My parents' answer to dealing with any crisis was, "Suck it up and get over it. Press on." We were simply not supposed to cave in. I suppose these traits were passed along through me to my children. So Natalee sucked it up and, limping to the tryouts with her leg taped up, she earned a spot on the Dorian dance team.

The Dorian girls at Mountain Brook High School were good friends as well as dance teammates. By her senior year in high school, Natalee had danced for four years alongside many of the same friends with whom she would graduate. These girls did everything together, from studying to dancing to traveling. Several of Natalee's friends would always accompany us on our annual family beach trip. Matt would take a friend too, so as not to be so painfully outnumbered by the giggly girls! The last time all the girls were together for this trip was the year before they graduated. It was the summer of 2004, and there's a beautiful picture of them together from that trip. It's a photo that has appeared in the media many times.

It was only a couple of months after this beach vacation, in October 2004, that Natalee came to me to ask about the senior trip that everyone was talking about. Many in the senior class had signed up for the exotic four-night trip to the Caribbean island of Aruba. Senior classes before hers had taken the trip. It was a tradition. Her stepbrother, George, had even been on it. And this year her stepcousins, Jug's nephews, who were also seniors, were going on the Aruba trip. Natalee really wanted to go, and if I could manage it financially, I really wanted her to have that experience, because she deserved it. She had worked very hard for so long. She was awarded the President's Scholarship at the University of Alabama, as well as a couple of others, for her outstanding academics. I decided that if I could swing this trip for her, I would do it.

As plans were being made, I attended two parent meetings with Jodi, the travel agent who organized the Aruba trip for this class as well as in the past and whose own senior daughter was also scheduled to go this year. At the meetings roommates, payments, and other details were discussed. The position of the chaperones was made clear. They would be there for emergencies such as lost passports, missed flights, and so forth. They would not be conducting bed checks and roll call. More than one hundred of Natalee's senior classmates were going to be on the trip in addition to the seven adults. It was comforting to know there would be safety in numbers.

As the New Year rolled in and 2004 became 2005, Natalee began planning for her senior trip. The minute the swimsuits hit the shelves we hit the malls. I specifically remember how torn she was over a cute little polka-dot suit. Does it look okay? Does it fit right? She was partly excited and partly anxious. Either way, she could not wait for the big adventure with all her friends.

As spring blossoms started to peek out from the azaleas in our front yard, Natalee began working on her graduation plans. May would be here before we knew it, and there was a lot to do. As expected, Natalee handled all of the graduation requirements and arrangements herself. She ordered her invitations, her cap and gown. Family and friends of Mountain Brook graduates have to have tickets to attend the ceremony, and those are always hot commodities around here. Typically, each family receives only six tickets because of limited seating, but Natalee worked hard to acquire enough for her entire family to be present. It mattered to her that everyone be invited. She called around to other seniors to find out who didn't need all of their tickets and collected as many as she could. This was going to be her big night, and she wanted all of her loved ones around her.

Natalee was ranked twenty-fifth in her class of approximately three hundred, and that's with a 4.17 on a 4.0 scale. Even with all her good grades and advanced placement classes, the competition within the school meant there were still twenty-four students with grade point averages above her 4.17. And she never let anyone forget the ".17" part! For her academic achievements she received three honors cords to wear around her neck with her graduation robe: a gold one for the National Honor Society, a blue one for Mu Alpha Theta, which is the Math Honor Society, and a red one for the Spanish Honor Society.

Those cords are worn proudly in the photos that have been seen in the media of Natalee standing in our front yard with her friend Liz. The two of them are in their graduation gowns. They were planning on being college roommates.

Only partly joking, I always told Natalee she could be anything she wanted to be as long as it was a doctor or a lawyer. Postgraduate work was already a given. Because she was so driven and hungry for achievement, she expected Matt and me to be the same. Sometimes we didn't measure up. I knew it was pointless to argue with her when we got into disagreements. There was no yelling involved, but it might be best described as passive-aggressive behavior on her part.

She could be tough, and very strong-willed. Matt and I always joked with one another about knowing when to stay out of her way! But in my eyes she always made good decisions. There were never drug, alcohol, or boyfriend issues with Natalee. It sounds too good to be true, but that's just who she was. She was unique.

In the weeks leading to graduation and the trip to Aruba, we also shopped for dresses for her to wear for sorority rush at the University of Alabama. Greek life is a big deal there, and Natalee was excited about getting into the sorority scene. We found two beautiful little sundresses that would be perfect for her to wear at the social parties. I vividly remember one afternoon about two days before she left on her trip when we were out shopping. I was looking for the opportunity to have a woman-to-woman talk with her about the nature of this trip, and our outing provided the perfect chance to remind her of the things that all parents tell their children as they transition into young adulthood. These are the same lessons parents teach their children all their lives: stay with your group and don't go with people you don't know, don't leave your drink unattended, and don't get into a situation or condition where you can't choose your free will and make your own decisions. Students Natalee's age are somewhat caught between that healthy fear of danger their parents teach them about as they're growing up, and complacency. They're too old to be guarded by adults all the time, but too young not to be reminded that there are dangerous people and dangerous places in the world. Natalee was almost grown. She was about to leave home. But I still reminded her to keep her personal safety as her first priority.

"Natalee, I'm a little worried about what you might encounter in those establishments in Aruba. I know when you're down there you're of legal age, but I want to remind you that men of all ages are going to find you attractive. They might try to approach you. Someone might even try to put something in your drink."

She acknowledged my warning with the typical teen reply, "Mom, I know. I know. I'll be careful ..."

Natalee had never had a boyfriend per se, as in going steady, or "going out," as it's referred to these days. But she had plenty of "friendboys," as we called boys who were just friends. At Mountain Brook High School it seemed most of the boys and girls were part of big groups. Only a very few had actually paired up as couples. Natalee and I always talked very openly with each other about sexual matters. She confided to me that she was a virgin. And I let her know that I was very glad about that. I continued my lecture and explained that some men might try to engage her. "People who go on these exotic trips are generally there to have fun, but there are others who may have another agenda. You could be a target. They might try to get you drunk and take advantage of the situation. You need to be on your guard at all times and stay with people you know." It would be very difficult to identify a time when Natalee was *not* with her friends. She was *always* with her group. We joked about how they all traveled in a pack. She promised to be careful. And I had absolutely no reason not to believe her.

Parents teach children about the dangers of the world not to make them live in fear, but because it's just not safe anywhere anymore. It might not be safe in your own home on the Internet in a chat room, and it might not be safe on an exotic island trip with a hundred friends. I made sure Natalee heard me when I warned her to guard her personal safety.

A former Mountain Brook student had returned from his senior trip to Aruba two years prior and told about an experience he had in the popular nightspot there called Carlos 'n Charlie's. Some locals were trying to get a couple of his female classmates to leave with them when this young man stepped in. He said he believed that he had helped abort a potentially dangerous situation. My recollection of his chilling account of this experience gave me my first feeling of apprehension about the trip. Natalee and I discussed what happened to this former student, and I felt better after reminding her about the possible dangers she could face. She had proven to be very responsible all of her life. I trusted her to be able to take care of herself.

As the countdown to graduation and her senior trip ticked down, the time moved very fast. On Friday night Natalee danced at the senior prom. The following Tuesday night she walked across the stage and accepted her high-school diploma. Two days after that she left for Aruba. And by the next Monday morning she was missing.

———————

ON THURSDAY MAY 26, 2005, Natalee came into my bedroom at three o'clock in the morning to tell me it was almost time to go. Everyone was gathering at a friend's house for the ride to the airport. My job was to pick everyone up at the airport when they returned on Memorial Day, Monday, May 30, 2005.

While Natalee was going to be out of town, Jug was going to his lake house to visit with his family and friends. In our marriage, the second for both of us, we rarely vacationed together. My son, Matt, had made his own plans with friends for the weekend, so it was the perfect time for me to take a much-needed, overdue trip to my family's lake house in Hot Springs, Arkansas. I had not been there in a very long time. Birmingham is about nine hours away, so it was just too long a drive since moving here to make the trip on a regular basis. I was very much looking forward to visiting with my family. Everyone's plans were made.

In the wee hours on this Thursday morning Natalee and I loaded her things in the back of the car and headed off to her friend's house. It was very dark at that hour, and we were both only half awake. But we did talk some. Small talk. We reviewed what she had packed, going through a mental checklist of passport, cash, camera, sunscreen, and the like. When we arrived at her friend's house, she came to life. The adventure she had been excitedly awaiting for months was finally about to begin. She jumped out of the car and bounced to the back to get her bag. I got out and walked around the car to help her. She gathered her things and looked up long enough for me to kiss her on the cheek.

"I love you! Have a great time!" I told her.

She replied, "Bye, Mom! Love you!" and slung her purple duffel bag over her shoulder.

The bag made her walk slightly bent to its opposite side. I got back in the car as she made her way up the long walkway to the front door. Turning the car around to leave, I stopped and looked back over my shoulder to see her go inside. The front door of the house opened just wide enough for her to slip in. I saw her silhouette in the beam of light that shone from inside. The light narrowed as the door closed, then disappeared completely. It was pitch-black again. I drove away not knowing that would be the last time I would ever see Natalee.

I'M GLAD I'M ALONE TO RECOUNT the events that have brought me to this place on this morning, preparing to pack up and leave this house and Mountain Brook. Standing in the doorway of Natalee's room, I unwillingly step inside to the center of it, look around slowly, take it all in. In what feels like slow motion, I bend my knees until they touch the floor, rest my hands on the light cream-colored rug in front of me, and roll over onto my right side. Curling up in a fetal position, my head tucked down, arms crossing over my chest, I close my eyes again. And the cry I have fought off for almost two years finally comes. The final good-bye cry. And it comes hard. From somewhere deep, deep inside me. And it feels as if it will never stop. As if the pain can never be contained again.

The Call

Anyone can predict it will be standing room only at the Reynolds lake place on Memorial Day weekend. The whole family gathers here every chance we get. My father built this house a few years ago, not long before he passed away, after the first one burned down. We might have been more upset about the fire, if that first house hadn't been so old. Vagrants had moved into it in the wintertime and had left a fire going in the wood-burning stove. The only thing left was the metal spiral staircase, set right in the center of the house. Not one shingle survived. In Hot Springs, Arkansas, on Lake Hamilton the only firefighting force was made up of volunteers. Apparently, word of the fire didn't spread as fast as the flames. By the time anyone noticed that the Reynolds place was ablaze, it was too late. The little cottage Matt and Natalee had visited since they were born and had enjoyed countless summer days in all their lives was gone. But it wasn't long before the new one was built in its place.

Hot Springs is about an hour and a half from Pine Bluff, where I grew up with my two older brothers, Paul and John. Weekends consisted of family excursions to Lake Hamilton, which was located in the town of Hot Springs, known for its natural, bubbling springs that are hotter than a Jacuzzi. Too hot to really enjoy. When I was a toddler my parents put a house trailer on a lake lot, and we left Pine Bluff every Friday afternoon during warm weather to spend weekends on Lake Hamilton. I learned to water-ski when I was four years old, surely being enticed with the challenge to keep up with my big brothers. Many years later when I was in high school, Mom and Dad were able to afford their first lake house. It was a small, simple, yellow house, outdated even then. Complete with 1960s dark teal green shag carpeting, it was saturated by that familiar musty lake-house smell. When it burned, we lost precious nostalgic things that were important only to us, such as our "butt skis," the use for which is self-explanatory. But losing that house gave my parents the excuse they needed to build a new one. Dad did most of the work himself. Certified as an electrician, he was talented as a jack-of-all-trades. He didn't even move the old metal spiral staircase. He just built the new house around it.

It's wonderful, and my children love their grandparents' new retreat. The rebuilt house is rustic, with cedar siding. It's cozy and charming, very warm and comfortable. Much larger than the old one, the new one has plenty of room for all the cousins and friends who join us every weekend in the summers. Typically at least eight double beds are always occupied, and the floors are covered with people in sleeping bags.

Long holiday weekends are the best. On Labor Day, Memorial Day, and Fourth of July breaks the place is full. We relish our time there, cooking, talking, taking boat rides, waterskiing, and playing games. Mom doesn't want us to eat out. She and I cook and clean up after every meal for all those visitors. And they are *real* meals! Spaghetti with salads, chicken tetrazzini, rolls, vegetables, the works. And occasionally hot dogs and hamburgers. Mom spends the weekdays cooking for the weekends. Each morning everyone is awakened by the inviting smell of bacon frying. I can still put myself there if I stop to think about it: waking up to the hum of a passing boat on the water close by and smelling that bacon. Somehow Mom always managed to get all of us together for breakfast, lunch, and dinner on Saturdays and Sundays. As I look back on it, it was a remarkable feat of wonderful fellowship. These are the happiest times for me, and for my children as well.

———————

IT'LL BE GOOD TO SEE MY FAMILY and just relax after all the hectic graduation and trip-planning activities. Natalee left for Aruba yesterday. So today, Friday of Memorial Day weekend, two friends, Marilyn and her sister-in-law Linda, will pick me up for the drive to Hot Springs.

When we get to the lake Mom has already prepared the meals, and the lake house is bustling with laughter and conversation among family and friends. It's a beautiful weekend on the water. Boats are out everywhere. People are water-skiing. I enjoy visiting with relatives I haven't seen in awhile. Everyone who didn't make it to Birmingham for the ceremony wants to know about Natalee's graduation night. They all ask about her exciting trip to Aruba. And I promise to send pictures to everyone when she gets home.

Every time I get to this lake house I just completely relax. There's something about being near the water and taking in some fresh air that revives a person. And there's so much personal history here. It's comfortable and inviting. Sitting lazily in a big chair out on the dock, I find all my worries seem to be put on hold until I'm back on the road toward home and headed back to reality. For now, it's just good to unwind. We eat lunch and visit well into the late afternoon. In the evening Linda and Marilyn opt for a hotel room because of the crowded house. It's just like old times. Every bed is taken, and bodies of all ages crisscross the floors in sleeping bags.

SUNDAY, LINDA AND MARILYN pick me up at the lake house around mid-morning. We enjoy lunch with the family before gathering our things to head off for some shopping along the main street in Hot Springs. In town, directly across from Bathhouse Row, where the bubbling hot springs are, there's a line of small quaint shops. But these weren't always little shops. Behind every door there used to be nightly live auctions going on. One after the other, all in a line down the street, you could hear the rapid-fire voices of the callers. Back in the 1960s our family would drive over to Hot Springs after dinner just to sit and watch the auctioneers. It was our form of family entertainment. All kinds of things were for sale. There was jewelry, furniture, pottery. There were paintings and antiques. We never bought, just watched. My brothers and I had to keep quiet and sit very still during the auctions. One scratch of the nose could mean we had just purchased something! I remember sitting on my hands on several occasions.

Other landmarks on Bathhouse Row are the Arlington Hotel and Madam Trousseau's Wax Museum. Matt and Natalee posed for pictures with every wax figure in that place. And did so on many occasions.

As the day lingers on, Marilyn, Linda, and I are so comfortable in our leisurely state at the lake that it's hard to think about leaving. But we know it's time to get moving if we're going to shop and then begin our nine-hour drive back to Birmingham.

The family accompanies Marilyn and Linda out front. I'm inside for a moment all by myself, grabbing a few last things, as everyone says their good-byes outside. In the upstairs kitchen I notice a yellow drink hugger on the table. Huggers like this one migrate in and out of this lake house with the numerous visitors who pass through here. But for some reason I'm compelled to walk over to it, pick it up, and turn it over. In small green letters across the bottom it reads "Carlos 'n Charlie's." Right then a powerful force runs through my head from the back of my skull all the way to my eyes. It's like my energy is going into the hugger as the hugger is coming to me. I immediately put it down as if I've touched something hot. I feel uneasy and slowly back away from the table, making my way down the old metal spiral staircase to the front door to leave the house. I'm not sure why I feel such trepidation at this moment. I believe now that what I experienced was a premonition. And it was my second feeling of apprehension about the trip to Aruba.

I take a few deep breaths and walk out to the car, reminding myself that this is the last day and night of Natalee's trip. She will get on the plane in the morning. I ask God to keep her safe for the journey home. I'll be back in Birmingham in time to pick everyone up at the airport at ten-thirty tomorrow night. Natalee will be home in a little more than twenty-four hours, I tell myself. I'm looking forward to seeing her. I miss her.

Marilyn, Linda, and I say good-bye to everyone and leave the lake house to browse the shops in Hot Springs. Being there always brings back fond memories of the auction days. We stay way too long, leisurely moving from one little shop to the next, but we're having such a nice afternoon just piddling around that it's hard to get in gear to make that long drive home. We're three working women who desperately need this short break. Our children and husbands are all occupied with their own activities this holiday, so we're doing the best we can to stretch out our carefree weekend.

In one little gift shop I find a complete set of *Wizard of Oz* figurines. Natalee will absolutely love this. They're beautifully fashioned pewter characters of Dorothy, the Tin Man, the Cowardly Lion, the witch, Toto, the Emerald City, the yellow brick road, and every other piece you can imagine. It's amazing how lifelike the little figures are, their faces delicately crafted with extraordinary detail. They're beautifully accented with tiny rhinestones and crystals. This will be Natalee's going-away-to-college present. Every single piece except, that is, for Dorothy's house. Since Natalee will be leaving home soon after she gets back from Aruba, this will serve as a symbolic recognition of her newfound independent living. I will give her everything except the house, because after all, *there's no place like home*. Marilyn buys an entire set for her daughter as well, including the house.

It's late when we leave the shops in Hot Springs to start the trip back to Birmingham. We get as far as Memphis, Tennessee, when we grow tired and decide to stay the night there. We'll get up to-morrow, on Memorial Day, to make the rest of our way home.

Rested and refreshed, we leave Memphis late Monday morning with Linda driving and Marilyn up front with her. I take the backseat. We sail along, chatting like we always do, talking about our plans for another road trip one day soon. Marilyn and I are happily speculating about what our daughters' reactions will be when they open their presents to find a set of extraordinary *Wizard of Oz* figures. Natalee will gasp with excitement when she sees these. Before we know it, we've crossed over into Mississippi. Somewhere amid our conversation, between the chuckles and the small talk, my cell phone rings. I don't recognize the number, but answer it anyway, which I usually don't do.

It's a young girl. "Mrs. Twitty? My mom … umm … my mom, she umm … wants to talk to you." It's the daughter of Jodi, the travel agent. She developed appendicitis right before the trip, so she and Jodi didn't get to go to Aruba. They are in Birmingham. It seems like an eternity before Jodi takes the phone.

"Tell me what's going on," I say in a voice much firmer than the one I usually hear coming from my mouth.

She simply says, "Natalee didn't show up this morning to get on the plane."

And instantly I know. It's more than a mother's intuition. It's certainty. Something terrible has happened. I have just answered the proverbial dreaded phone call that no mother or father ever wants to receive. The one we fear from the moment our children are born. The one that changes a parent's life forever.

———————

JODI'S WORDS INSTANTANEOUSLY transfigure my relaxed state of mind into one of intensity and grave anticipation of what she is going to say next. Stunned, I ask, "What do you mean she didn't get on the plane?"

Jodi explains that the students were to meet in the hotel lobby this morning to board the buses for the airport. At that time Natalee's roommates notified the chaperones that she didn't return last night. There's no sign of her. Her three hotel roommates have not seen her since their outing last night. No one knows where she is.

It's surreal actually saying the words out loud, telling Linda and Marilyn that Natalee didn't show up for her flight this morning. That she is *missing*. They hold it together for a few minutes while I call Jug. I ask him to see about getting transportation to Aruba right away. He hesitates, saying maybe she just simply missed the flight.

"C'mon, Jug. You know this isn't like Natalee. She might be early for something, but *never* late. Please! Please see what you can do!"

Linda is running off and on the road. She and Marilyn are crying. Linda's daughter died a few years ago, and surely those horrific memories are surfacing fast.

My mind immediately goes into overdrive to try to figure out how to get from this spot on the interstate somewhere in Mississippi to an island called Aruba. Think! Think! I remember that Martee, one of my teacher friends, was recently talking about a friend of hers who is a private pilot. I call her and ask her to put me in touch with this person. I'm explaining to her what's going on, that Natalee is missing, and look up to see myself in the reflection of the rear passenger window, leaning slightly against it, the cell phone to my ear. The treetops become a blur against the sky. And I witness myself saying, "Is this how it happens, Martee? You just get a call? Is this how it happens?" We hang up, and I pray the first of a million prayers. I ask God to give Natalee the strength to endure, if she is alive, until I can get to her. Ask Him to hold her and protect her. And to give me the same strength, so that I can endure the painful thoughts and sickening heartache and work diligently to reach her.

Talking to Martee is the only moment of sadness I allow myself. From this point on I get control of my mind. I have to. I know instinctively that it's up to me to take the actions necessary to find out what happened to Natalee. I have to get tough and suck it up, and I do, because she is depending on me.

All three of us are on our cell phones all at once in the little car trying to find someone who knows someone who is a pilot or who has a plane. We receive a couple of replies that because it's Memorial Day some pilots who have been contacted have already "popped a top"—consumed alcohol—and cannot fly. It's not looking good, and Linda continues to run off the road.

"Pull over, Linda. Pull over right now! Let me drive!"

Taking the wheel of this car, I step on the gas and don't let off 120 miles per hour as we blaze down the interstate toward Birmingham. In the left lane with the flashers on, I periodically sound the horn to warn other drivers who might dare to cross over in front of me. We just filled up with gas. We can make it a good ways before we have to stop again. The car is performing remarkably well at this speed.

This is not overreacting. Natalee is missing. She never leaves her group. They travel in a pack! How did this happen? She needs help. I am sure of it. The scene is frenetic, yet I'm not frenzied. With a cell phone propped between my ear and one shoulder, a pen in one hand writing on paper being pressed against a knee, and the other hand on the steering wheel, I continue working on getting information. My heart isn't pounding. My fist isn't clenched on the steering wheel. In spite of the circumstances, I experience an indescribable calm. I'm hyperfocused. Quiet, not yelling. Somber. Yet I can eat metal with my teeth. Perhaps it's controlled terror. Keeping my mind in check and my heart and emotions suppressed is paramount, because I know if I let go for just a split second to evaluate what is really happening, I will cave in. I have to stay calm to get help for Natalee. Missing her scheduled departure time is so out of character for her. Something is terribly wrong. I have to get to where she is. Find her. And bring her home.

Calling 911 repeatedly, I tell them about my daughter. Ask for an escort from state troopers. Confess that I'm driving 120 miles per hour and not going to slow down. Ask them not to pull me over. They want to know where we are. We report the mile markers and exit numbers as we fly past them. But those become a blur and practically illegible at the speed we're traveling. Over and over I call 911 for assistance. Call Jodi for more information. My son, Matt, calls. "Mom, this is serious. You gotta call somebody like the FBI." He's right. I try. And try again. But it's a holiday, and no one is on duty in the Birmingham Bureau office. Matt calls back with more phone numbers. He and his buddy Hunter are working feverishly to gather all the information they can think of. We talk about every three minutes, so he can provide more numbers.

All three of us in the car engage people at home to get on the phones to find help. Something. Anything. As word spreads among the families of the other students on the trip many parents pitch in. Friends call the FBI and the U.S. Embassy in Washington, D.C. Natalee's friends, awaiting their departure from Aruba, collect the remaining long-distance calling cards from the group. Exchanging numerous calls with me they desperately try to communicate everything they know about where she was last seen and with whom. Natalee's friends don't want to leave the island without her. Liz and Frances Ellen say they will stay until I get there. I become emotional. There's discernible fear in my voice as I accept their offer. Then the girls get emotional. But after thinking about it for a moment, I tell them all to get on the plane and get out of there for their own safety.

One of the chaperones, a coach, is staying behind in case Natalee happens to come back to the hotel. He doesn't know what to say to me. Maybe it's shock. He's working on getting information on Natalee's last-known whereabouts. I ask him to stay in the hotel lobby, so he can see her when she comes in. And so she can see him, and know that she isn't alone.

The next call I make is to the U.S. Embassy in Washington, D.C. I tell whoever answers the phone about our crisis. We talk about three minutes, then hang up. Desperate for more help, I realize I need to speak to someone in an official capacity. So I call back and talk to a vice-consul for almost fifteen minutes to report our crisis and give all the information I have. I feel relieved after talking to this individual, knowing now we'll get some help. The very next call I make is to Natalee's cell phone to leave her a voice message. "Natalee, hang in there. Help is on the way. Please call me. I love you." This is pointless, but it makes me feel better. Natalee doesn't have international calling on her phone. We haven't talked to each other since she left.

Crossing into Alabama, we zoom past a state trooper who is traveling in the opposite direction. As expected, he flips around to pursue us. I back off to 110 miles per hour to allow him to catch up. I constantly check behind me, hoping to see him close in. His blue lights are reflecting in the rearview mirror way back in the distance behind us. We've been moving at this speed for some time, and the car is burning gas at a faster rate than it probably would under normal driving conditions. We need gas, and finally pull over so the state trooper can either write me a ticket or arrest me. Or both. It was never my intention to outrun him, just to keep running.

He pulls up close behind us, blue lights flashing. The tall, slender officer cautiously gets out of his car and walks up to the back of ours. What must he be thinking? Are we running from the law? Are we robbers or drug dealers? Surely all the training he has experienced in his career is coming to the forefront of his thoughts. As he approaches the car, I get out and walk toward him. I'm relatively calm, yet he raises his open palms toward me at about his hip level and tells me to stop. So I do.

Then Linda and Marilyn fly out of the car and start toward him shouting, "Her daughter has been kidnapped! We need help! We need help!"

He raises his open-palm warning to shoulder level and gives his command in a slightly louder voice. "Stay right there."

All three of us keep coming.

As a final warning he raises his hands almost over his head, palms pushed out toward us, and says loudly, "All of you, *stop!*" He probably thought he was going to have to shoot three women right there in broad daylight on the side of the road.

Linda and Marilyn are asked to get back in our car. When they do, the trooper puts me in the car with him. The first thing he does is make me look at his radar. It reads 110 miles per hour.

So I start explaining. "My daughter has been kidnapped in Aruba," I say as I try to remain calm, focused, and coherent. Kidnapping is the only conclusion we can come to right now.

I also tell the trooper that I've been trying to reach the FBI office in Birmingham and that the man who answered the phone said no one is there today who can help us.

"That should never happen," he says, "even on Memorial Day," as he works on locating the phone number for the FBI in Washington for me. He hands me the piece of paper with the number on it and says firmly but in a very nice tone, "Ma'am, you're just going to have to slow down."

So I do, driving 85 miles per hour the rest of the way home.

Continuing to trade phone calls with the students who are waiting to fly out of Aruba, I get the tip we need. The Mountain Brook students were at Carlos 'n Charlie's on their last night on the island. Natalee had been there with her group. Dear God. Carlos 'n Charlie's. The intuition yesterday after seeing the hugger. The very same nightspot a former student told us about where girls were being enticed to leave with men they didn't know. The students say Natalee got into a silver or gray Honda with a young man who had befriended some of her classmates. One of Jug's nephews, Thomas, says he actually met the guy Natalee was seen leaving Carlos 'n Charlie's with. He said he played poker beside him at the Excelsior Casino, which is located inside the Holiday Inn, where the Mountain Brook group was staying. Thomas says this young man's name is "Gerran or Juran or something like that." Thomas isn't concerned that this guy would do harm to Natalee. "He just seemed like one of us, y'know … a regular guy. Like me."

The last information communicated from the students before they board their plane is that this Joran guy is a tourist from Holland. And he is staying at the Holiday Inn.

———————

THE THREE OF US ARE STILL on the phones in the car when we finally get to Birmingham. We screech to a halt in front of the house and run inside, where I learn friends have secured a private plane. Okay, I'm thinking, we have a fighting chance. It's a huge relief to know I can get down to Aruba so quickly, because time is of the essence. Natalee has already been unaccounted for since about one-thirty this morning. About fifteen or sixteen hours now.

We need to be at the airport in an hour. In the bedroom I put a few things in a bag. Jug still doesn't want me to go.

"She'll turn up," he says with certainty, trying to reassure me.

People are gathering at the house, but I don't really notice. I go into the kitchen and sit on the floor in a corner. My back is against the glass French doors that lead out to a wooden deck, knees pulled up to my chest. Macy the dog is right beside me. She knows something is wrong. I'm aware that people are staring at me, but unaware how focused I really am on thinking about what to do. Now that I don't have the driving to concentrate on, it's apparent that I'm in a very unique and unfamiliar state, a very trancelike, deep-thinking zone. I'm all by myself, but not alone. Tears roll slowly down my cheeks. I sit in silence. Praying. Praying. The sounds around me are like the "white noise" on those machines some people use to help them sleep. I don't talk. The others discuss who will accompany me on the plane. The decision is made. Jug, Jodi, and two fathers of other girls who were on the trip, Mat and Ruffner, will go with me. Waiting to go to the airport is the longest hour of my life.

On the way out the front door I grab Natalee's beautiful senior portrait from the small sideboard in the foyer and reach over and take the one of her in her dance-team uniform off a table in the living room. Clutching both portraits, Jug and I drive to the private hangar at the far side of the Birmingham airport. On the way I contact Cingular Wireless and have international calling activated on my cell phone. I activate Natalee's too. If she has hers with her, she can call me now. If she had had international calling last night, she could have called someone for help. Why didn't we do this before she left? I feel such regret. And sadness. She may have been in a bad situation and couldn't call anyone. Why, Lord, didn't we activate that service? The students will be home in a couple of hours, and I will be able to communicate with them from Aruba. Other than the discussion with the cellular operator, there is very little conversation on the fifteen-minute ride to the airport.

Having this transportation made available to us so that we can get to the island so quickly is a blessing and a godsend. If not for this extraordinarily generous gesture, we would have to wait until tomorrow to leave for Aruba.

I've never been on a private plane before. As we approach the aircraft and walk up the few steps on the ladder and into the cabin I don't even notice if it's pretty or special or anything. I go straight to the back and take a seat away from everyone else. I don't want to talk. Have to think. It's understood by everyone that we're on a mission to find Natalee and bring her home. Not one of us thinks we'll be coming back without her alive. But there are unspoken concerns regarding the condition in which we might find her. Has she been raped? Is she being held against her will? Has she been drugged? Dearest God, what has happened to my child?

No one says much at all on the four-hour flight. Continuing to make calls for information as long as I can get cell service in the air, I talk again to the coach. He says he may have found a U.S. Drug Enforcement Administration (DEA) agent who can help us, but is having trouble connecting with the police on the island. He's having a hard time getting past the beach patrol and getting to the "right authorities." Then we lose contact.

A small radar at the front of the plane shows we're passing the Bahamas. Passing Haiti. The Dominican Republic. Finally we inch toward a landmass that looks as if it could be the island. Aruba looks very tiny. We can do this, I think. We can find this Joran guy, and we can find Natalee. But first we have to find the right authorities. How hard can that be?

Everyone Knows Everyone

There is nothing we can do until we land in Aruba to search for Natalee and this Joran fellow. Thinking about how to go about this consumes my thoughts. Over and over in my mind I try to put the pieces together of what we know. She got into a car with a young man named Joran, or something like that. Why would she do this? Did she think she was getting into a taxi? She has never left her group before. Was she forced? Was she taken while in an altered state? Was she able to make her own decisions? Had she befriended someone she grew to trust? We just had our mother-daughter talk about such dangers a few days ago. She couldn't have forgotten our discussion, and let her guard down. She couldn't have forgotten the experience told by the former Mountain Brook student about his encounter in Carlos 'n Charlie's. Surely his story about how he thwarted an attempt by some men to coax his female classmates out of that bar crossed her mind as she made plans to go there last night.

No matter how this happened, I know this for sure: she is being held against her will or she has been murdered. And either way it's not by her choice. I go over the possible scenarios, careful not to let my heart and emotions take over. Thoughts of her and what she might be going through or what she has gone through have to be pushed aside so that I can keep my mind intact. For a moment, however, I let go and begin to think of the worst things that may have happened to her. My thoughts begin rushing uncontrollably. Guilt, second-guessing the decision to let her go on this trip, horror at the thought of where she is and what is happening to her, fear, regret for not adhering to my apprehensions. These emotions consume me all at once. It's frightening. And paralyzing.

A parent just knows when something is wrong. Natalee has never in her eighteen years exhibited any behaviors that even remotely resemble missing a scheduled time. I let her go on this trip because she earned it. She promised to be careful. She's on the threshold of adulthood now. But maybe I shouldn't have let her. Maybe she was too vulnerable and naive. But she is so responsible. She makes good decisions. What has happened? My thoughts are unclear, jumbled. I'm on the edge of panic. "Take some breaths," I tell myself. Mustering my strength, I suck it up and regain mental control.

It's around eleven o'clock on Memorial Monday night when the island comes into full view. I'm shocked by its land size. I had imagined a small exotic island with a few tiki huts bordered by beautiful beaches. I really don't know anything about the place or what to expect. It looks and feels like we're approaching

Atlanta at night. How will we find Natalee down there? It's much bigger than what I envisioned. Overwhelmed and discouraged, again I must quickly refocus. All the while holding on very tightly to her portraits.

We land, and the door opens. The heat and the humidity hit me hard in the face even at this hour. Like opening the oven door and getting that big hot blast. The wind is whipping. My hair is all over the place. I can hardly see the steps to go down. I soon learn this is how it always is here: very hot and very windy. "Hellish" is the only word that comes to mind.

We walk a few feet into the processing area to show our passports and go through customs. It's a small unimportant looking structure with a porch connected to the front of it. The owner of the plane has arranged for "handlers" to meet us here to assist with customs and ground transportation, common practice when private planes arrive in Aruba. Two men, Alberto and Claudio, are assigned to us. A third person, a woman named Eldrith, joins them. The three seem genuinely interested in our plight and begin asking a lot of questions. I show them Natalee's picture and tell them all that we know at this point about the bar, the silver or gray car, and the young man she was last seen with, named Joran. We decide the best place to start is at Natalee's hotel, the Holiday Inn, located in an area of the island known as Palm Beach in the capital city of Oranjestad.

An official-looking American woman in the processing area draws my attention. Her badge identifies her as a U.S. Homeland Security Office representative, and I hone in on her like radar. The sight of her is our first real sign of hope. I walk over to her and have to restrain myself from grabbing her by her lapels and pulling her into a hug to thank her for being here for us. All the calls made to the FBI and the U.S. Embassy by Natalee's brother and our friends must have paid off. That's why this official person is here to help us. I get very close to her and begin to tell her about Natalee and what has happened. Talking a mile a minute, I explain about Natalee's disappearance and our desperate situation. I ask for her help in figuring out where to start and what to do.

She never changes her stance, remaining in an "at ease" position with her hands behind her back. She has very little to say; volunteers no information. The encouraging thoughts that lifted me when I first laid eyes on her are quickly extinguished as I learn that she is always here. The Aruba airport is her post. She isn't here for us. She can't do a single thing to help Natalee. She has no special powers. No authority.

This is the first of hundreds of times along this impending tragic journey that hope would dissolve almost as quickly as it would appear. It would wash over us like the tide, then ebb. Hope comes, then goes. But it's the constant waiting for the next wave to roll in, and reaching for each new sign of hope that will keep us going, as it brings with it the energy and encouragement needed to press on in our search for Natalee, even if only for a few moments at a time.

All of us load up into the handlers' big white van and head for the Holiday Inn. We are foreign, desperate for help, and at a loss as to where to begin. Retracing Natalee's last-known steps makes the most sense. As we bump along in the crowded van on the potholed roads, I look side to side to take in as much as I can. There are a lot of lights, but not much activity. Passing the downtown district recognizable American store names catch my attention. We also pass a huge industrial and shipping area. On my left is freight car after freight car stacked three and four high, in numerous rows, all standing behind a tall chain-link fence. It's the cargo area of the shipyard. Seeing the stacks of empty freight cars makes me think about how many hiding places there must be on this island. I don't want to think about that right now. Just want to get to the hotel to meet with the coach and the DEA agent to find out if any progress has been made getting help from local authorities.

Along the way our handlers offer comforting words, saying, "Don't worry. Everyone knows everyone in Aruba. She will be found." They offer encouragement, saying that in Aruba no one wants to be the "black mark" who causes damage to the island's reputation. "If someone harms her, they will become the black mark, and that is bad, so they will not harm her." They continue to tell us a little about "One Happy Island," as the slogan reads on the license plate on the car in front of us. From the air the seventy-five-square-mile island looks like a sliver of exposed lava rock rising out of the Caribbean Sea that has broken off from nearby Venezuela. In fact, that country is fewer than twenty miles across the water from Aruba., beach to beach. I had no idea it was that close. Reports of drug cartels and human trafficking that come regularly out of Venezuela give me another cause for grave concern. It feels much more South American here than Caribbean.

The handlers speak a mixture of English and the island language known as Papiamento, which is a combination of Portuguese, Spanish, and Dutch. As difficult to understand as it is to listen to, Papiamento is spoken on all of the "ABC islands," as Aruba and nearby Bonaire and Curaçao are referred to. Aruba is in the realm of the kingdom of the Netherlands, but is an autonomous state. We learn that Aruba calls its own shots concerning matters on the island.

"Before there was tourism here, the island depended on oil refining," the handlers tell us. Crude-oil refining was the island's main source of revenue from the 1920s until the mid-1980s. Luxury hotels, casinos, and tourism soon took the place of oil.

It's hard for me to believe that it's still the same day I was on my way home from a wonderful family weekend at the lake. I'm supposed to be picking up Natalee and her friends at the airport in Birmingham right now, not in Aruba looking for her. We arrive at the Holiday Inn, get out of the van, and go inside the open-air lobby of the hotel. The coach and DEA agent are to our left, and we turn to walk toward them. Suddenly everything in my line of sight is overpowered by the image of Natalee's purple duffel bag sitting on the table next to him. My knees weaken as I continue to walk toward it and the coach. Staring at the bag, I don't reach over to it. Don't touch it. Can't. Her things immediately become sacred to me. The coach said he was uncomfortable leaving everything in her room unattended and brought her things to the lobby with him.

I go straight to the DEA agent and begin telling him what we know. How there is nothing about Natalee's history and character that would explain why she is missing. How she has never been in any kind of trouble. I figure the best thing I can do is help this agent understand who she is.

Following our brief conversation, we all walk immediately to the front desk to ask about someone named Joran who is staying in the hotel and plays in the casino here. The Holiday Inn night manager, Brenda, knows him by name. "Oh! Yes … yes … Joran. He gambles in the Excelsior Casino here. He likes to prey on young female tourists. Especially the blonds. He is tall. Good-looking boy. Like a Dutch marine." My mouth drops wide open.

"Where is he from?" I ask her.

She replies, "He lives in Aruba."

I stutter, "He's … he's not a tourist just here for the summer?"

"Non, non," she says.

"He isn't staying at this hotel?"

"Oh, non! Non, non …"

It takes a few moments to absorb this information. The supposed tourist who befriended some of Natalee's classmates and who told them he was staying at their hotel lied to them. He isn't a tourist. He isn't staying here. I experience a sinking feeling. My heart is in my throat. But I'm so perplexed by this revelation that I can't really process it. We try to figure out how to see what Joran looks like. If he isn't a guest here, then we have to figure out a way to find him, so that once we locate the police, we will be able to show them who Natalee was last seen with. Jug's nephew, Thomas, said he played cards with Joran in the casino. We ask if there are videotapes of the blackjack tables. Brenda at the front desk says that, since the Excelsior Casino operates sepa-rately from the hotel, it will be difficult to locate someone at this hour to show us the footage from last night. Maybe tomorrow. The Excelsior Casino is owned by an American named Michael Posner, who has reportedly been associated with a well-known crime family in Chicago. Posner has been convicted of criminal activities in the United States and came to the island a few years ago to open businesses including casinos, hotels, and restaurants. We also ask the manager for the records that show who entered Natalee's room last night. Those will have to be pulled for us. So we turn to the coach to catch up on information.

Apparently, finding the local police *was* hard for him. The coach tells us that he was led to believe that the beach patrol of-ficers he had been dealing with since Natalee disappeared were the "real" police. But they aren't. The beach patrol did not contact "official" authorities. They didn't feel it was an urgent enough issue to request that a police report be filed. The Holi-day Inn manager did not contact proper officials. Everyone just shrugged it off, suggesting that Natalee will return on her own. "Just wait for her. She will come back," they reassure us. I'm trying to understand this. Maybe they don't realize what we're saying: *someone is missing*. It's very frustrating that no one will take any action or offer any help. Perhaps this is just how they do things down here. All of us are dumbfounded by this blasé atti-tude. No one would direct the coach to island police authorities or give him any helpful information. So he kept vigil in the lobby. He was at a complete loss until the U.S. DEA agent sur-faced on the island.

It's hard to comprehend that the beach patrol and the hotel staff won't pay attention to a tourist's crisis. Maybe that's how they keep their crime reports looking so good. By ignoring crimes and victims, they can say they don't have any. By looking the other way, they can claim Aruba is a safe haven for tourists. The coach has not been able to even meet with an official to have a police report filed. Natalee has been missing for close to twenty-two hours now. A crime may have been committed. But it has not been officially reported or documented. The only reason we can come up with for being ignored is that this tragic event will make the island look bad. Give it a black mark. But I was not about to let this get swept under the rug.

The DEA agent asks for Natalee's cell phone and passport. I don't want to reach into her bag, but I don't want anyone else to touch it either. A little carry-on purse is attached to the side of it. Inside are her passport, cell phone, and some cash right on top. I remove them and zip the purse back. The agent looks at Natalee's things a few moments, then gives them back to me. I return Natalee's things to her little purse as I walk back to her hotel room to leave her bag there. Seeing her passport is a sign of hope. At least she hasn't left the island. She's here somewhere. We can find her. When I return to the lobby the DEA agent suggests we go to Carlos 'n Charlie's to ask questions and show her picture around. So we load up and head back to the shipyard area.

Carlos 'n Charlie's is very close to where the cruise ships dock. It appears to be just a few yards away. Another wave of grave concern takes my breath away for a moment. Has Natalee been taken away on one of these ships? Discarded at sea? Taken to another country to be a slave? Sold in the human trafficking market? Rushing negative, horrible thoughts have to be controlled.

Making their way inside the bar the men dodge a couple of fistfights and dope-smoking patrons to try to find someone with information. They don't learn anything, so we all load up again and drive to a nearby gas station, where the DEA agent wants to introduce us to someone associated with the island cell-phone company to help us get phones and set up communications among our group. The man is named Charles, and he arrives in a beaten-up rental car. "My silver Mercedes is in the shop" he feels the need to explain.

While the men are talking, Charles asks me to get into his car with him. He is some kind of self-proclaimed clairvoyant and thinks he can help find Natalee if I will just cooperate and answer a few questions. I've never been one to put stock in black magic, psychics, and crystal balls, but faced with this kind of desperation and urgency, it's amazing what one will endure in reaching for the next sign of hope. What if Charles can help us communicate in more ways than by island cell phone? Who am I to doubt he might have some special magical powers that will tell me what has happened to my daughter? Completely at his mercy and open to anything and any help I can get, I can't risk not cooperating with him. But I should have known better.

Charles tells me to close my eyes and think about what Natalee's face looks like. "Don't open them," he says.

"Okay, I won't," I whisper.

He begins to ask very personal questions.

I don't answer.

"I detect problems. How is your sex life?" He asks probing questions that make me very uncomfortable. More appalled than frightened, I open my eyes and tell him that I cannot continue with this, as it has nothing to do with finding my daughter. Jodi walks up to his car just in time and gets in with us as we wait for the men to figure out what to do next.

Back at the Holiday Inn we again ask management about watching the video of their blackjack tables to see what Joran looks like. This time the hotel manager finds someone to show us the tapes. Jug and I will view the tapes while the handlers volunteer to hit the streets to see what they can learn. They ask for some cash to buy information. Without hesitation, Jug gives them a couple hundred dollars.

It takes about an hour to facilitate seeing the security footage. Scrolling through the videos we see images of Jug's nephew, Thomas, and immediately call him. He tells us he was sitting with Joran at a blackjack table at the Excelsior Casino last night, Sunday night, before everyone went to Carlos 'n Charlie's. He describes the young man and the clothes he was wearing. We see Thomas and stop the tape. Over the phone we tell him what we see. He begins to describe Joran and where he is sitting. And bingo, there he is. Now we have a mental picture of him to go with his first name.

Excited, Jug and I run down the stairs from the casino toward the lobby and almost collide with the handlers, Alberto and Claudio, as they run into the lobby toward the front desk. Alberto is waving a piece of paper. "We have him! We have him and the car!" The two of them are as exhilarated as we are. They have Joran's last name. It's van der Sloot. And they have his address. The two have been around to beaches and bars on the island asking questions. They paid beach bums a hundred dollars to tell them about someone named Joran and about this silver Honda.

I would soon learn that, despite the barriers between Papiamento, Dutch, and English, everyone here speaks the universal language of money. You can buy almost anything in Aruba: services, information, sex, and drugs. The same is true in the United States, but it's just more blatant here and appears to be more acceptable. And everyone here seems to operate on some kind of underground communication system.

People know everything that's going on on this island, whether they will tell you about it or not. That must have been what Alberto meant when he said, "Everyone knows everyone." The beach bums told the handlers who the person is we're looking for and where to find this car. How in the world could a couple of beach bums know all this? I think to myself. Alberto and Claudio went to the location, looked over the fence, and there it was. A silver-gray Honda with big tailpipes and fancy features, just as the students had described. They wrote down the license plate number and the address. On the piece of paper is everything we need: the name of Joran van der Sloot, his address, and the tag number of the car Natalee was seen getting into. Soon we will know the owner of this car.

"We need to go back to that house with the police," I say, thinking that I'm in America and that we need to at least try to follow some kind of law enforcement protocol. We haven't located any police yet, but with this solid information (the name, address, and tag number) the handlers decide to take us to the Noord police station. It's the closest one to the van der Sloot residence. Finally. I know now we are going to find out what has happened to Natalee. We have the car and we have the person she was last seen with. He knows where she is. All he has to do is tell me, and we'll get the hell out of here as fast as we got here.

Overwhelmed with anxiety and anticipation as we drive to the police station, I feel like I want to climb out of the moving car. I want to hold her. Get her home. Help her heal from whatever she has been through. We'll spend the rest of our lives in therapy if we have to. I just want her back.

At Noord it takes almost half an hour to get uniformed officers to accompany us to the van der Sloot home. Once we arrive, Mat and Ruffner, the two men from home, go around to the back to make sure no one tries to leave. Jug gets out and goes to the front with the officers. The silver Honda isn't here anymore. I remain in the car on my cell phone with Natalee's friends who are back home now and gathered at one of their houses. Staying in the car will keep my temper in check. If I get face-to-face with the young man, I will lose it. Anger will dominate me. I don't want to hamper the police work by flying off the handle. The officers sound their horns and sirens for about five minutes before a man answers the door. He is Joran's father, Paulus van der Sloot. He has his cell phone in his hand. The police ask to see Joran. Paulus responds that he isn't home and calls his son to find out where he is. He tells the police that Joran says he is in a poker tournament in the back of the casino at the Wyndham

Hotel. Again we load up, adding Paulus to this madcap posse riding in convoy with the police to the Wyndham. Charles the clairvoyant is in his car and continues to follow us around. Half of our group is traveling in a white van, the other half in a rental car. The police car leads the pack.

On the way I plan how to beat the father to his son. I decide that I am going to nail this kid right there in the Wyndham casino and confront him about my daughter's whereabouts. Ask him why he lied to the Mountain Brook students about being a tourist. Why he lied about being a guest at the Holiday Inn. All of these hotels are lined up one after the other in the Palm Beach area of the island, so it doesn't take long to go from one to the next. We arrive at the Wyndham, and the car barely stops rolling before I jump out, and literally run through the police officers and Paulus to be the first one in the casino. Frantically I look left and right and left again, asking the pit bosses if they have seen Joran. I run straight to the back where Joran told his father he would be and return to the front. There is no sign of him. I turn around to see Paulus on his cell phone again. He tells us that his son is back at their house now. He is there with his friend, Deepak Kalpoe, the owner of the silver Honda.

Meanwhile, during this casino invasion, two Wyndham Hotel security guards report that they saw two dark-skinned males and a tall white male with a blond girl out by the beach a few hours ago. Could these be the men who took Natalee? Our group splits, and the men run in two directions to the back of the Wyndham and out to the beach area. I remain in the lobby with Paulus and the police. Natalee's portrait is in my arms. My fingers are white from holding it so tightly, as I wait with the hope that the men will walk back in with her. But they don't.

The scenario gets wilder, and tempers get hotter. We are instructed to go back to the van der Sloot residence, where Joran is now waiting. Everyone is rushing and running to the cars. Few words are spoken. We arrive to see people standing in front of the house. They are Deepak Kalpoe and Joran van der Sloot. Deepak is dark-skinned. Maybe he's Aruban, I think. Joran is white. Maybe this is who the guards at the Wyndham were talking about a few minutes ago. The Aruban police, Paulus, Jug, Jodi, Mat, Ruffner, the coach, and I wait for the DEA agent to arrive. The DEA agent tells everyone to remain in their vehicles until he gets there. And suggests that the women not get out of their cars at all. Jodi stays in the van, and I stay in the rental car, on the phone with Natalee's friends. They're on a speakerphone, guiding me with information.

One of the boys from home describes Deepak's car and the people in it to a tee. There were two Arubans in the front, and Natalee and the white guy in the back, he tells me. He says it was chaotic when everyone was leaving the bar. It closed down earlier than anyone knew it would because it was Sunday night. Everyone was scattering to find a cab. Most of the taxis in Aruba are unmarked or poorly marked privately owned vehicles. Natalee's friends wonder if she thought she was getting into a taxi with Joran. She shouted out the window to her friends who were still in the Carlos 'n Charlie's parking lot, "I'm going to ride back to the Holiday Inn." Then she shouted, "Aruba!" That was the last time anyone saw her.

The DEA agent arrives, and all the men gather in a circle in the dirt and gravel driveway area under a streetlight in front of the van der Sloot home.

The police lean against their squad car several feet behind Joran. The scene looks like a cheap one-act play in a small town theater on a dramatically lit stage. And I'm in the audience. Joran and Deepak have supposedly returned from a night of gambling at the Wyndham. It's about three o'clock in the morning. It's a school night. They aren't dressed as if they have been to a casino. They are in grubby T-shirts and shorts. I make a mental note that I will ask to see the casino footage from the Wyndham later on. Just to see if they were really there tonight— or, rather, this morning. Alberto and Claudio go back and forth between the group and my car to update me on the conversation.

I'm watching the scene unfold as the silhouettes weave anxiously and nervously in and out of their circle, talking. Joran is asked about being with Natalee last night. He says he met her at the blackjack table at the Excelsior Casino at the Holiday Inn on Sunday evening. Her friends were making plans to go to Carlos 'n Charlie's later that night. He met up with her again there. Natalee was dancing when he got there. He says he did Jell-O shooters off of her stomach. He ordered a "yard whiskey coke" and bought Natalee a shot of 151 proof rum, a very potent liquor. It was frightening to hear this, because I'm sure Natalee didn't know the strength of this drink. He says she drank it, and then she had to have some of his "whiskey coke" to wash it down. He says Satish Kalpoe was standing right next to her when she did this. We learn that this is Deepak's brother, and that he was the fourth person in the car with the rest of them. We learn that Deepak and Satish are from Surinam.

Joran said Natalee wanted to go with him when the bar closed down, so they got into Deepak's car, Deepak and Satish in the front, he and Natalee in the back. He says she yelled "Aruba" out the window to her friends, and they yelled back for her to get out of the car. But Joran says she wanted to ride around. Then before he continues he asks if anyone in the group is related to Natalee. Jug steps forward and identifies himself as her stepfather, and Joran asks him to walk away, so that he can finish telling about his encounter with her.

As Jug leaves the encircled group and comes over to the car, Joran resumes his story. He says he and Natalee were in the backseat of Deepak's car and that she asked to go see sharks. He says he told her that they don't have sharks here, but she insisted. So he says they took her to the lighthouse, describing how they made out in the backseat on the way there. He says several times that "she was so drunk!" He says she kept falling asleep and waking up. Falling asleep and waking up. He describes crazy things she said, such as she's a lesbian, she's related to Hitler, and a few racist remarks. It's excruciating to imagine what my daughter endured on this car ride, if indeed she was even conscious at all.

Joran describes Natalee's underwear with the dark blue embroidery and the flowers. He describes her pubic area. I know what he is referring to. She is shaven higher than usual for her bathing suit. Dear God. He *has* been with her. Joran continues and tells the men that he inserted a finger in her. Then another one. I am sickened by his sexually explicit and graphically detailed account. Nauseated. And I am embarrassed for her. Natalee and I have always talked very openly and frankly about male-female relationships. She hasn't had a boyfriend yet per se. Joran says she is a willing participant. But he says he decides that she is too drunk to continue this encounter and returns her to the Holiday Inn.

Paulus interrupts his son, telling him not to say anything else, telling him he does not have to talk to us. They speak in Dutch to one another. Mat and Ruffner become agitated, saying they doubt Joran would act so nobly as to stop this sexual encounter to return her to her hotel. Paulus becomes angry and starts shouting that we, in responding to his son's vivid and illicit account, are somehow out of line.

"No jurisdiction! You have no jurisdiction!" Paulus shouts. "He does not have to talk to you! You have no manners! No manners!"

"We'll show you some manners. Just tell us where the girl is," retorts Ruffner. "We came a long way to find Natalee, and I have a serious problem with you, son, because you admit to being the last person with Natalee. You should tell us where she is."

Joran responds arrogantly, "Fine. What would you like me to do?"

The conversation is deteriorating, and we can't get any more information. Everyone is very tense, and it's moments from coming to blows. With all this yelling, the Aruban police, who have stayed outside the ring of fire, step in, telling everyone that this is the end of this confrontation. We are to disperse. Alberto walks over to my car and reports that Joran and Deepak insist they dropped Natalee off at the Holiday Inn. I relay this to the students back home who are still on the phone with me. They shout back, "No, he didn't drop her off there! He is lying!" They are telling me to go inside the house. They can hear the shouting between Paulus and the others. They hear the chaos.

"Go inside that house, *please!*" they shout. Everyone feels that she must be inside, either held captive or incapacitated, and that I should go inside. I ask. But the police say they have to have a search warrant to let me in. I ask again. Paulus, a judge-in-training, knows exactly what he has to do and exactly what he doesn't have to do. And he knows that he doesn't have to let the police or me inside his house. And he refuses.

As we stand there in the wee hours of Tuesday morning, May 31, 2005, waiting to get a search warrant that is never obtained, the two who were last seen with Natalee offer to show us where they dropped her off early yesterday morning. For the last time we drive back to the Holiday Inn, where Joran and Deepak demonstrate with great detail where they took Natalee, and how she stumbled and bumped her head getting out of the car, describing her over and over as "so drunk." I watch from the car, holding Natalee's picture close to my chest. The group moves inside the lobby, where Paulus and Joran lose control, yelling very loudly at everyone in the group in Papiamento or Dutch. The police make them leave the lobby. Paulus and Joran come to the car where Charles the clairvoyant, Deepak, and I have been sitting. Joran and Deepak then show me exactly where they dropped Natalee off in front of the hotel entrance, spreading their arms in illustration of the area, which is right outside the front entrance of the Holiday Inn lobby.

The car door is cracked open about a foot to let air in. The intense heat is pierced with a cold hard stare from Paulus to me. And I give it right back to him. Next Joran squats down by the slightly open door and comes close to me. I hold up Natalee's picture and say to him, "I want my daughter back. *Give her back.*"

Popping his chest with an open palm, he says, "What do you want me to *do*? What do you want me to *do*?"

By his words, countenance, and body language, I take this to mean that it's too late. There is nothing any of us can do. He doesn't say, "I don't know what happened to her," or "I have nothing to do with your daughter's disappearance," or "I'm so sorry.... How can I help you?" And a sickening feeling washes over me.

The reenactment is over. The van der Sloots and Deepak Kalpoe leave. The police leave. The others in our group from home check into their rooms to get a couple of hours of sleep before sunup. Jug and I are staying in Natalee's room. He goes for some rest before we will go to the police station to give our statements. I'm going to wait in the lobby for the police detective named Dennis Jacobs to meet me. He is supposed to be here in a couple of hours. I certainly can't sleep. Maybe Natalee will just walk in. I wait in the lobby alone for the detective and review what just happened.

From the time we landed last night, we have been from the airport to the Holiday Inn, to Carlos 'n Charlie's, back to the Holiday Inn, to the Noord police station, to the van der Sloot residence, to the Wyndham casino, to the beach behind the Wyndham Hotel, back to the van der Sloot residence, and now finally back to the Holiday Inn. We stood in the front yard of the young man last known to be seen with Natalee and were not able to secure a search warrant to go inside his house or look in his friend Deepak's car. I fear that she might be in that house or, worse, in the trunk of that car. But the police were right there with us. They're in charge. We trust that they'll do what has to be done. But they can't get past the would-be judge. And it's apparent right off the bat that privilege and political standing will present a much greater obstacle than the language barrier ever could.

———————

OUR LIVES WERE ABOUT to be shaken up in ways that will be very difficult to communicate because they are so unbelievable. We are about to encounter chaos way beyond the experience of this first night. We have no way of knowing that we are embarking on the world's most horrendous wild goose chase, one the whole world will witness. We could never have predicted the events and the characters that will be revealed before us. What happened surrounding Natalee's disappearance is bizarre enough without having to be contrived or embellished. If I had not lived this myself, I might even question some of the circumstances in the story that is about to unfold, so I'm glad that others were present at every strange twist and turn to witness the occurrences. Many times those close to Natalee's case have said to one another, "You just can't make this stuff up."

Not in Kansas Anymore

L ast night's meeting with the DEA agent would be the last time we would see him. I was told he was just on the island "on vacation," but considering his line of work, I have to wonder about that. Even wonder if the name he gave us was really his. None of that matters. I'm just thankful he was here when he was to help us get the ball rolling by directing us to go to Carlos 'n Charlie's, and helping us with the encounter in the van der Sloot front yard. But now we're alone, politically and law enforcement–wise. Even though we've met Homeland Security and DEA representatives, there's nothing they can do for us. There's no U.S consular office here. No State Department representative. No FBI agent. We're on our own and will have to rely on local authorities to initiate the investigation into Natalee's disappearance until help arrives. We've called all the offices in Washington, D.C., and all the senators and representatives from Alabama, even the governor himself. Surely help is on the way.

I feel the heat of the sun coming up as I wait in the lobby for police detective Dennis Jacobs. It's getting hotter with every minute that passes, and I'm anxious for him to get here. Even this early the breeze through the open hotel lobby is quite warm. The humidity is already very high. Daylight comes, and I see the island for the first time. It's paradoxical to see such beauty and experience such horror at the same time.

Something out of the corner of my eye moves and catches my attention. Adjusting my focus I zoom in on the biggest iguana I have ever seen! It's moving slowly along the sidewalk, where it encounters another lizard. The two of them lazily swing one leg forward at a time, tongues tasting the hot wind, and travel down the walkway ignoring the tourists around them who stop to point and stare. They're all over the place down here. Everywhere I look there's one or two or three. Giant colorful lizards and smaller versions as well look like little dinosaurs and are free to come in and out of the facilities all over the island. This is a miniature Jurassic Park, my tired mind says to itself. Island visitors who are up early to enjoy the day come upon the iguanas and take pictures and ooh and ahh. But big lizards leave big calling cards that dot the sidewalks, and one must watch where one steps. Hotel guests hopscotch the droppings.

Typical resort scenes come into view as the hotel awakens. People with large hats and sunglasses. In sandals, swimsuits, and shorts. Some much too fair to be out in this intense tropical sun. Cameras dangle from necks, wrists, or shoulders. Children chase each other around the pool. I look beyond these scenarios to the blue-green Caribbean and the soft cream-colored beach and see the water for the first time. And the infinity. Instantly, I'm dizzy. And turn back around quickly. My head swirling. I can't look toward the beach and into the vastness of the sea. Can't bring myself to look where there is no ending in sight. It's too limitless. It feels as if I will lose control if I look at the water. I need boundaries. Need the land and the perimeter to hold me in. And, yes, it crosses my mind that Natalee could be out there somewhere. In the water.

The side of the island where these upscale hotels are located is the smooth-water side. There's almost no current. Only an occasional wave laps the shore, courtesy of a small passing boat. The other side of the island, where tourist attractions like the coral rock Natural Bridge and the Cave are located, is the rough side. It's said that if something is placed in the water there it will disappear in the current forever. It's hard to look in the direction of the water. It's many weeks before I can.

Detective Dennis Jacobs arrives and takes a seat on a sofa in the lobby across from where I'm sitting on a coffee table. The officer, uniformed in black pants and a black shirt, pulls his notepad out of his pocket and takes his pen out to write. This is a welcome sight. I feel more secure having the police take charge of this critical situation. It must mean that now we're in good hands. Maybe we'll get somewhere.

As Americans we have faith in the police process. When something goes wrong and we're in trouble, we pick up the phone and call 911. We're confident that someone on the other end of the line will come help us. We rarely think twice about whether anyone will show up, because we know someone will.

We're spoiled with the expectations that we'll be treated with fairness and respect by law enforcement authorities and that justice will prevail. But expecting it to be like this everywhere around the world is terribly naive. And I am about to find out what it means to be involved in a crisis outside the United States. It's just as Dorothy said to Toto: "We're not in Kansas anymore."

I'm certainly glad to see the officer. Relieved that someone in an official capacity appears to be taking an interest in Natalee's disappearance. But expressionless and seemingly unconcerned, he asks to see her passport and her driver's license. I show him her passport and the cash that I found on top of it when I removed it from her purse last night. I want him to see that she doesn't have anything of value with her. I explain to him that since her driver's license is not in her bag, we all assume that she has it in her possession. The detective asks if she has a debit card or a card for teller machines. Natalee didn't bring her debit card to Aruba, and I explain that it's at home. I know exactly where it is in her purple-painted curio in her bedroom. But I can't prove it. And for some reason he doesn't believe me.

Detective Jacobs asks us to come to the police station in Bubali in about an hour to give our official statements. Bubali is his post and is in the opposite direction from the Noord station, where we were last night. There seem to be ample police stations on the island. So why didn't the beach patrol or hotel staff contact them when Natalee was reported missing?

When the detective leaves, I go to the hotel room to get Jug. Jodi is also going with us. We meet Mat and Ruffner in the lobby a few minutes later on their way to take a cab out to the lighthouse to see what they can find out. Joran said last night that Natalee wanted to see sharks there. We leave the hotel in separate directions.

Jug, Jodi, and I arrive at Bubali at eight o'clock sharp. One of the first things I notice is Deepak Kalpoe's silver-gray car parked in the back. It's definitely his. I spent a lot of time staring at it last night. The tag. The details. Not sure what to make of this, I mentally prepare myself for an encounter with Joran van der Sloot and Deepak Kalpoe inside the police station. And maybe I'll also get a look at the other guy, Satish. We proceed through the gravel and dirt parking lot and enter the front of the small, sea-foam green stucco building. It's clean inside and reminds me of a doctor's office. We walk across the hard-surface floor to the waiting area. To my left are a half dozen or so blue plastic chairs. Above, the ceiling is vaulted, and there are offices in a loft setting. Glass and curtains separate the people working up there from the noise below. Detectives and police officers in the loft can look down to see who is in the reception area. In front of me is a short counter with a half door that swings. And farther to the right beyond that are a few officers working at their desks.

Detective Jacobs is sitting behind the counter in a reclining swivel office chair. As we move toward him, he leans back in his chair. "We're ready to give our statements," we say, anxious to tell him the facts about Natalee's disappearance we've gathered thus far, so that an investigation can get under way.

He pushes one hand and then the other down and across his belly, which is extended by his rearing back. He says, "I'll have to eat my frosted flakes first," and then, running a hand across his jaw, adds, "and get a shave before I can deal with you." And with that he gets up from the chair, exits through the little swinging door, and disappears.

We are speechless. And have no recourse but to sit down and wait. A half hour passes. Then an hour. I wish there was an American law enforcement contact here to help us, someone to act as a liaison. I get up from the plastic chair, go outside, and sit down in the gravel driveway. Despair is weighing in on me. Trying to stay mentally focused, I can't help but begin to sink. The profound lack of urgency and disinterest for my daughter and what has happened are incomprehensible. We're in serious trouble. Helpless. I'm outside about thirty minutes when another officer, police chief Jan van der Straten, comes out to the driveway and tells me bluntly and curtly to get up.

"You can't sit in the gravel like this. Come back inside."

Inside, two more hours pass. If this is a tactic to break me down and make me give up, it won't work. If I'm supposed to throw up my hands, leave this building, and go back to the States without Natalee, they'll have to do a lot worse than this to douse my hopes of finding her. After almost three hours detective Jacobs comes back into the waiting area and tells me he doesn't need me today. He won't take our statements today. What? I don't understand. Did the young men give theirs? We never see them, but Deepak's car is still outside. Are they upstairs in the loft area? Can they see me? Numb, I turn and walk out of the police station, out into the gravel again, barely able to navigate the little stones.

Alberto waits by the van. There are a cameraman and a reporter with him from the local Aruban television station. Alberto knows we are in trouble. Leading me to the camera, he says, "You need to go on TV."

I'm a preschool teacher of children with special needs. My life is quiet and modest. I've never been on TV and don't have a clue how to do this. But I'm not at all fearful about it. Just driven to plead for help. What should I say? Where do I look? At the lens? At the reporter? How does this work? Will it be broadcast here and on nearby islands? What about Venezuela? Maybe Natalee will see me and know we are desperately trying to find her. I don't know where to begin, but a prayer is answered as I open my mouth and begin to speak. The words somehow just come as I tell the reporter about Natalee and how uncharacteristic it is of her not to be on time for her flight, how dependable and accomplished she is. I describe what she was wearing when she disappeared and where she was last seen, then hold up our two cell phones. Directly into the camera, directly to her, I say, "Natalee, I have my cell phone and yours. There is international calling on both of them now. Please call me." Clutching her portrait and the two phones, standing next to Jug outside the Bubali police station in the bright hot sun, wearing sunglasses and the same clothes I have had on since I left Memphis, I give my first ever television interview.

Alberto takes complete charge and initiates media contacts for us. This consumes the rest of today. He takes us to all the media outlets to get the message out about Natalee's disappearance. Spreading the word is our focus, and even with Alberto's guidance it's quite trying, because everything takes a very long time to accomplish. Alberto and Claudio suggest we go to the

Aruban newspaper, printed in Papiamento and Dutch, called *Diario*. The man who owns it, Jossy Mansur, owns a lot of businesses and properties on the island. In the most profound category of "it's a small world," Jug learns that Jossy's sons attended the same American military school that he did. After another hot, bumpy drive in the van from the police station, we arrive on a backstreet area of Aruba. It's very industrial-looking all around us. Alberto leads us into the *Diario* office.

It reminds me of a junior high school inside. It's painted soft colors, and there are big metal desks. People are working in small spaces. There are sounds of keyboards and typewriters and voices speaking in indiscernible foreign languages. Phones ring. It's busy in here. And comfortably cool. We make our way down a narrow hallway, pass a few reporters at their desks, and sign in at a window where a woman has family photos on her desk. Her pictures calm me. She is warm and friendly, in stark contrast to the cold treatment we just received at the police station. She seems to know what to do. We all pile into this woman's office to give her information. It's crowded, but we are never made to feel uncomfortable. The *Diario* staff lets us use their computers and charge our cell phones. I begin to feel like perhaps we can make some headway here.

The *Diario* newspaper will run a story tomorrow about Natalee's disappearance. The staff ask for photos and gather pertinent facts such as where she was she last seen and what she was last seen wearing. To get the last-known photo of Natalee, I contact her friends back home. We ask the students to check their cameras to see who has the most recent photo that might show us what she was wearing at Carlos 'n Charlie's Sunday night. I'm anxious to see what they have. Everything takes so long!

Finally, after a couple of hours, the photo arrives by e-mail. And there she is. It's hard to look at, yet I can't look away. She's happy. She's with her best friends as they pose together on the last day of the trip. I look long and hard at Natalee, standing on the far left end of a line of friends along the shoreline. It's the photo they took before they went to Carlos 'n Charlie's two days ago. Natalee has on her favorite denim skirt and a colorful teal and white top we shopped for together just before she left home. My eyes are fixed on this photo when I realize she is on the beach. The sea is behind her. The tide is at her feet. I already can't look at the water; now seeing this photo makes it even more difficult. Maybe the water is another premonition, or maybe it's recognizing the obvious and dreaded question that will soon be asked over and over: Is Natalee in the water?

After spending a lot of time with the *Diario* staff on details and facts, they are kind enough to e-mail the photo to the nearby print shop. We'll go there next to design posters, which will include Natalee's picture and a tip-line phone number for people to call in with information.

We drive a short distance to the print shop. Inside we summon help from an employee and begin to lay out a poster that reads "MISSING." It appears surreal. Dreamlike. *That's my daughter who is missing.* My actions are mechanical and practically imaginary as I hand over the phone number that will accompany the new photo. The poster reads that Natalee was last seen yesterday at one-thirty in the morning at Carlos 'n Charlie's. We place an order for a hundred posters. It's getting well into the afternoon, and I want to get some of them up in the store windows before closing time.

The work that needs to be done is teaching us how to do it. It feels good taking these steps and moving forward, as it becomes clearer that it's up to us to initiate some action. And staying busy is a good thing too. It gives me hope. If I can keep putting one foot in front of the other, maybe we'll get someplace. And maybe I can keep from caving in.

Alberto leads the way again and drives Jug, Jodi, and me to a TV studio and a radio station to record pleas for Natalee's safe return. The television facility is very nice and well equipped. We walk past a newsroom and the studio where they do live broadcasts. A reporter is all set up and waiting for me in a side room. The microphone sits on a coffee table, and I'm tempted to constantly lean down toward it as I give the details of Natalee's last-known whereabouts. The interview lasts only a few minutes, and Alberto whisks us off to a radio station, where I give the same information again live on a radio show. All the while I'm wondering if Natalee can see me or hear me. I want her to know how hard everyone is working to find her. I want her to hang on.

My son, Matt, calls during all of this hurried running around to media sites. When I tell him what we're doing by broadcasting Natalee's disappearance here on the island, he says he will contact CNN. God bless him. He is a world away and wants to do something to help his sister. And in a short while I receive a text message from him that reads: "Mom, I called CNN in Atlanta and told them about Natalee, and now the whole world knows."

Maybe Matt has the right idea. His message makes me think that perhaps getting the word out everywhere *is* a good idea. So I call my friend Sunny in Birmingham, the only person I know who is in television. A freelance writer and producer, she tells me there is already a lot of "chatter" in the local newsrooms about the missing Alabama girl in Aruba. But because the high-school personnel and the students aren't talking, none of the reporters know any details yet—not even Natalee's name. At my request Sunny arranges for me to do a news report by phone to air on our local Birmingham FOX news channel, WBRC. But before we do it, she wants to make sure I understand the consequences.

"You know, once you open this gate, Beth, you can't close it, so be sure you're ready," she explains, trying to help me understand the potential for the story to go national, even international, in a matter of just a couple of days. Sunny also expresses concern that if someone has Natalee and wants to make a deal for her return, they might do her harm if the story appears on the news.

"Let me speak to whoever is with you," she says.

Jodi takes the phone and explains we've already recorded some news reports here.

And Sunny says, "Well, then it's already out there."

"Let's do it," I say.

We're in the rental car on our way to the lighthouse. I need to see it. See where the locals claim to have taken Natalee. The roadside view out from the populated resort area is dotted with houses, then becomes scant, until finally the terrain is solid with nothing but dense shrubs, some cut off at the same height by the unforgiving wind. As we approach the lighthouse even the shrubs disappear and the surrounding area becomes barren. There's nothing here. Just hot sand over hard lava rocks and a lighthouse. It sits on the cliff at the tip of the island. The very tip. It's extremely windy here. The whitecaps on the sea are visible just beyond the edge of the cliff, and water sprays crash against the rocks below. As we approach the lighthouse in the car, I'm on the phone recording my first American news story about Natalee's disappearance. I see the lighthouse, but don't look beyond it to the water.

The interview will air soon on tonight's evening news at home, Tuesday, May 31, 2005. But when I hang up with the reporter I begin to have second thoughts. I'm torn between needing to call in all the help I can find and needing to be extremely cautious. But what if tourists who visited Aruba last week are back at home in the States and remember seeing something? Anything? Anyone? Maybe Natalee. What if other tourists remember seeing the individuals in question on the same snorkel trip Natalee took? There might be valuable information out there that can only be gathered by using the news media to our advantage. But what is the right thing to do? After recording all the interviews on the island today that should be enough for now, I conclude. Nervous and still second-guessing this decision, I call Sunny back to tell her I want to cancel the report I just did. Change my mind. Leave the story on the island and not let it out in the United States yet. She exhales into the phone through pursed lips and responds that she will try to have it pulled from the local newscast. After another few minutes of anxiously thinking it through, I realize we have nothing to lose by asking the public for help and information and call Sunny again.

"Let it go," I tell her—and unknowingly light the fuse of a phenomenal media explosion.

————————

JUST BEFORE THE PRINT SHOP closes on this Tuesday evening we return to pick up the posters. The bright red letters that spell out MISSING across the top are startling. I really can't even believe this is happening. Immediately we hit the streets to hang them in store windows. Almost every storeowner is obliging. Armed with a stack of posters and a roll of tape, three of us make our way around the resort end of the island along the now brightly lit strip of restaurants and hotels. With each poster hung I think, she can be found. Someone will know *something*. Everyone knows everyone ...

We return to the Holiday Inn, where Mat and Ruffner are waiting to fill us in on their search today. What they tell us is like a scene out of a bad crime movie. Mat and Ruffner took a cab to the lighthouse this morning. They got out and walked around on the rough terrain of lava rocks and looked over the cliff into the extremely forceful current. They had a picture of Natalee with them, and as they searched, the cab driver, a woman named Trina, got out of her car and joined them as they walked around.

"You are looking for a girl?" she asked.

"Yes, we are," they responded, showing her Natalee's picture.

Trina told them they need to go to the "choller houses." *Choller*, we're told, is the name for the drug addicts on Aruba, and the choller houses are where they live. "All missing girls at choller house," she said with certainty. And with that, she offered to take Mat and Ruffner to the crack-house area near Carlos 'n Charlie's. These houses are five-tenths of a mile from that popular establishment and from the docks where the cruise ships land. Just one block behind the upscale shopping area. Right in city center.

Trina wouldn't let the men go in the choller houses by themselves. She said it was dangerous in there. Instead, she called one of the addicts to come out. For five dollars he took Natalee's picture inside and showed it around. Maybe someone would know something. Then Trina called another person for assistance. Mat called him "Big Man," a former drug kingpin who quit the drug business after becoming a born-again Christian. Big Man is valuable because he still has his old drug network in place. He volunteered to help because he says he himself saw a blond girl in one of these houses at four o'clock yesterday morning.

Big Man met Mat and Ruffner at a crack house to discuss the situation. He asked them if Natalee had any money or a debit card. I piped up and told them that the detective had asked me the very same thing this morning. The men knew Natalee only had a few dollars with her at Carlos 'n Charlie's and that her debit card is at home. Then Big Man explained the island crack and cocaine racket and how it works. He said that unsuspecting tourists are taken to the choller houses. He said the crack addicts pump the tourists full of the drug, then take their cash and their debit cards. Once all their funds have been used up and there's no money left, the dazed and confused tourists are left on the beach somewhere.

If all this is true, it's the reason the coach couldn't get any help. It's why the police are not in a hurry to put a lot of effort into finding Natalee. It's the reason the hotel managers just shrugged off her disappearance. No wonder everyone is so reassuring that she'll be back. They all think it's just another tourist abduction by island crackheads. *So they aren't going to search for her.*

Mat continues the review of his day, saying that Big Man walked through the first choller house himself looking for Natalee. He came back out to Mat and Ruffner and said, "They see me coming and they know how to hide. They move her. They move her. We come back tonight."

The silence that blankets our small group is impenetrable as the men recount their experiences. Deafening silence. I can't hear or feel anything. I'm empty and exhale a long breath that seemingly has no end. So this is commonplace? Is it automatically assumed that all people who go missing are being temporarily held captive in the drug houses? This is the first any of us has heard of this theory. The addicts have her. God help Natalee. And we call home to make arrangements for a medical evacuation plane to come to Aruba to take Natalee home when we find her.

After this meeting with Big Man, Trina drove Mat and Ruffner out to some fields on the far end of the island where crack addicts merely exist in lean-tos doing their drugs all day long. The government does not disturb the addicts in the fields or in the choller houses and in fact provides the structures for them to live in. "The government flags on the roof mean this is a government choller house," Trina explained. "They live here for free if they leave tourist alone. They do the crack all day."

There was no sign of Natalee in the fields or the choller houses today. I can't decide if this is good news or bad.

Trina will pick up Mat and Ruffner at ten o'clock tonight to take them back to meet Big Man again, and they will search more choller houses and go through brothels, too. The men did not want to tell me about this. They are as stunned as they speak the words as the rest of us are listening to them. I see the painful reluctance on their faces as they explain their encounters this afternoon. The task before them tonight is unthinkable, but they don't hesitate. Not for a moment. They are fathers, loving dads whose daughters were here with Natalee just a couple of days ago. They know that we could just as easily be looking for one of their girls. Their empathy is deep and sincere, and I am very grateful for their bravery and courage.

Tonight we are tense and quiet as the men wait for their ride to the choller houses and whorehouses. The mood is broken for a moment when I get an uplifting call from home telling me about the prayer service held for Natalee this evening at Mountain Brook Community Church. This isn't our home church, but it's where many of Natalee's friends go. Reverend Tim Kallam opened the church doors, and loving, caring people poured in to show their prayerful support for Natalee.

"We desperately need those prayers," I tell the caller. "Please. Everyone keep praying."

But I don't tell about the task that is before us in a couple of hours.

———

A FEW BLOCKS FROM THE CRUISE ship docks Mat and Ruffner meet with Big Man to begin their search. As they approach the first choller house, Big Man says that only one of them can go in with him at a time. Mat goes first. Inside, the chollers are all "cracked up" and screaming at the top of their lungs in Papiamento for the men to get out. Big Man knows what to do. He leads Mat through the passageways that connect the choller houses to each other and goes through each one exposing the hiding places inside. Some of the walls have false partitions. By swinging a sheet of plywood paneling to the side a secret hiding place is revealed. It's the wall cavity. There's a chair or two inside the wall. "A strange place for chairs," Mat observes. Big Man says people hide from the police here. And sometimes the chollers hide girls and tourists within these spaces. They must hide long enough to need to sit down.

Inside the choller houses are drugs and paraphernalia everywhere: pipes, needles, marijuana, cocaine, heroin, Ecstasy. There might be a mattress on the bare dirt floor where the wood has long since deteriorated. There might be an old school desk and a chair. And it's filthy. People of all ages are slung up against the walls inside. Men, women, children, young, old. They stagger around like zombies. They're angry, wild with drugs. Mat witnessed a lot of people coming and going, buying drugs. And he saw a lot of other things he won't tell us about.

As this guided tour of crack-house row is taking place, the tip-line phone begins to ring. The posters must be working! Around one o'clock Wednesday morning tips come in nonstop. We're all feeling very confident that we will have a chance to find Natalee as one call after the other tells us where she is. Our adrenaline is pumping hard. We run to the vehicles, directions in hand. Half of our remaining group goes one way to a gas station where a blond American has been seen, and the other half goes another way to check out a woman who matches Natalee's description. Neither tip pays off. But the phone keeps ringing. And that has to be a good sign. With every bit of information we think, okay, this is it. She'll be around the next corner.

Mat and Ruffner are now traveling the back roads with Big Man asking groups of people on street corners if they have seen Natalee. Big Man shouts out the car window, *"Chico Mericano? Chico Mericano?"* as he holds up Natalee's picture. At a corner drugstore they get a tip that she might be at a particular choller house they have not searched yet. It's worth a look, and again they follow Big Man into the underbelly of the happy island. And again, nothing.

"Check our whores! Check our whores!" shout the brothel owners as the men pass through each one. Looking into the faces of numerous prostitutes, young girls who carry cards certifying they are VD free for ninety days, they can't decide if it's good or bad that Natalee isn't among them.

————

IT'S ABOUT THREE O'CLOCK in the morning when the tips slow down. Jug and I are in Natalee's hotel room. I call my minister, Reverend Doug Carpenter, in Birmingham. His wife puts him on the phone in these wee hours, and he offers comforting words as best he can after being awakened like this. We agree to talk again later.

This is really the first opportunity to actually spend time in Natalee's hotel room. Her duffel bag is in the corner. I stop and look at it a moment, then walk over to it and, with eyes already closed, fall on it. Grasping it, I hug it hard, crying. The anger and frustration built up from the very long day are released through every tear duct. Every pore. I lie down in Natalee's bed, on her side, for about two hours. I don't sleep. I cry. And think how we can get a leg up on this incredibly desperate situation.

I have only my resources as a preschool teacher and my faith to draw from. I think about my precious students and how we diligently work on the same exercises and skills every day, watching and waiting for some glimmer of improvement. As a speech pathologist, I work with children with severe limitations. Some can't walk or talk. Each morning parents enter my classroom filled with hope and faith that they will return in the afternoon to see some little improvement in their child's quality of life. Even the smallest advancements are celebrated and give the parents great hope. Maybe that's how it needs to be approached here. Maybe we have to chip away at it slowly, take one baby step at a time, doing what we believe is right over and over each day. Repeating our pleas for help, remaining tenacious in our efforts, until there is some kind of result.

I don't know what to do. I can only do what I know. When daylight comes we'll do everything we have done all over again, starting with trying a second time to give a statement at Bubali police station. Then we'll put up more posters and replace the ones that have been removed. We'll get the word out in the media, chase the leads, meet with police. We'll do these things today and the next day and the next until there is an answer. Until we have Natalee.

The Statement

It's cold inside the Bubali police station Wednesday morning. At least it is to me. It's not that the air-conditioning is too high; the lack of food and sleep are affecting my physical condition. It must be ninety-five degrees at eight o'clock in the morning, but I am shivering, causing the plastic chair in the lobby of the police station to vibrate on the hard floor. I wait, wondering. Who is caring for Natalee? Does she have food and water, or shelter? Not knowing these answers, I consciously impose self-deprivation of food, sleep, and bathing. If Natalee can't rest, then neither will I. If she's hungry, I will be too. If she can't bathe, then I won't either. I fear the thoughts of the suffering she is enduring and push them back to address the task at hand.

Jug, Jodi, and I wait, again, to give our statements. The time is ticking away. An hour passes. Then another one. There's still no acknowledgment that we are here. I'm sure they see us from the loft above. For the life of me I cannot figure out the lack of urgency, especially if Natalee is being held in a crack house as

Big Man and Trina tell us. But we remain patient, respectful, still faithful to the police process. And finally detective Jacobs comes out to the waiting area to get me.

Detective Jacobs says he will only take my statement, not the others'. And I have to go alone with him. Jug and Jodi have to stay in the lobby. The detective and I walk toward the back to a small room where his cubicle is located. His desk is a table pushed up against the wall, leaving only three sides to it. There's a computer on the table. I sit in a chair that faces the wall. He sits to my right. The first thing I notice is a stack of torn papers on the table. The stack is torn once in half, then once again. It draws my attention as an official-looking document, but I don't realize what it is just yet. I sit down in the chair and draw my legs up to my chest, wrapping my arms around my knees. Shivering harder.

The detective takes a seat at his desk and sorts through some papers before getting ready to type at his computer keyboard. It's quiet. I am very cold, waiting for him to begin. As I stare at the torn documents on the table, the words *Joran van der Sloot* jump right off one of the ripped pages at me and pierce my eyes. It's Joran's witness statement, torn up, lying in plain view. So he has been here. He has given his statement. It has been destroyed for some reason. Did he change his mind? Can you even *do* that? Did someone come along and decide it wasn't in Joran's best interest to go on record about what happened to Natalee? I wonder if the father, Paulus, has been here. It's disarming. And I have so many questions about this pile of torn papers. But I don't know enough about law—certainly not Dutch law—to understand what it might mean to destroy a witness statement. All I know is now it's my turn to give one—finally.

At what seems like one letter at a time, Jacobs types in Dutch what I say to him in English. It's tedious. Arduous. Downright painful. It's a very, very, very slow process. I tell him about arriving on the island two days ago, on Monday night, and locating the last individual to have been seen with Natalee. I explain finding the car she was seen getting into parked at the van der Sloot home. I review the dramatic encounter in the van der Sloot front yard in the wee hours of Tuesday morning during which Joran described his sexual activities with Natalee as she was falling asleep and waking up. Falling asleep and waking up. How he described her as very drunk.

Describing the reenactment that followed at the Holiday Inn, I relate how Deepak Kalpoe and Joran van der Sloot specifically showed me exactly where they left Natalee. I give the names and include elaborate detailed physical descriptions of all those present for this demonstration. I tell how Joran and Deepak said she stumbled and bumped her head, how she refused help from them and went inside the lobby.

For two hours I talk. He types. Jug comes in to check on me. A little while later Jodi comes in, then leaves again. I am still talking, and the detective is still typing. I've been here for a total of four hours when we finally finish with my statement.

At the conclusion, Jacobs calls in another detective, a younger uniformed officer, and gives him some verbal directions in Papiamento. The young officer turns to me and begins to read my statement back to me, from Dutch to English. When he gets to the last word he looks at me and asks, "Are these your words?" And I respond to the affirmative. The statement is printed out, and I sign it. But I am not allowed a copy of it.

Jug comes back to the little office as I unwind my legs from my arms to get up from the chair, preparing to leave. Jacobs makes a feeble attempt to comfort us by saying, "You know … she'll show up. You should just go to Carlos 'n Charlie's, and a crack addict will bring her back when she runs out of money."

Shocked, I reply, "Wait a minute. The two young men who were last seen with her told us they left her at the hotel. Remember? I just gave you all that information. How they dropped her off. How she bumped her head. We just went over that! Remember? Besides, I already told you she doesn't have a debit card with her, and I showed you all her cash. It was in her bag. Whoever has her isn't keeping her for the money." And I softly divulge my worst fear—as if saying it quietly will make it untrue—that she is being held for sexual exploitation. Rape … Pornography … Torture …

Jacobs pipes up, "Oh! You don't have to worry about that! We have the *puntas* for sex. The drug addicts don't take the tourists for sex, just for money."

I look at Jug. We are thinking the same thing when Jacobs volunteers, "*Puntas*—whores. We have them, so Natalee is not being held for sex." Jacobs continues and describes the island crack scheme used on unsuspecting tourists, a story that is now all too familiar. It's the same tale told by Big Man.

According to Jacobs, the chollers take tourists to the crack houses and get them high on the drug. The victims of this scheme get all "cracked up" and then freely spend their money to buy more of the drug for themselves and others around them. Jacobs says that when the tourists' cash runs out, it's common for the crackheads to either convince them to use their debit or ATM card to get money for more drugs, or they steal the card when the individuals are incapacitated, threatening the tourists in order to get them to surrender their secret code. And when all the money is gone and the account is dry, the tourists are let out on the side of the road or often returned to Carlos 'n Charlie's. He maintains that Natalee is in a drug house on the island. He's convinced that when all her money has been withdrawn, they'll "put her out" on the beach or on the road.

I remind the officer again that we showed him Natalee's cash. She doesn't have any with her. I remind him that her ATM card is at home in her curio. She doesn't have it with her. And just in case I am mistaken, which I know I am not, I call the bank in Birmingham to see if there has been any activity on her card. It is confirmed that there has not been. And suddenly I realize that the detective is contradicting what Joran and Deepak told us and showed us last night. If they dropped her off at the Holiday Inn, how did she end up in a crack house?

I get colder. Shaking now. I want to wake up from this nightmare and can't. It's all so surreal. Staring at Joran's torn statement on the table, I walk out of the little office. Somehow I know right then and there that I'm up against way more than I have bargained for. The police want me to believe their island crackheads have my daughter and that she'll be released when they're through with her. And the statement of the son of a high-ranking justice department official is ripped up. Dear God, I pray. I need you now, and so does Natalee. Please, God. Help us. What do I do Lord? What do I do?

The day is half gone as Jug, Jodi, and I drive back to the Holiday Inn. It's quiet in the car. My mind is holding together by its last dendrites of mental capacity. I try to think what to do. Think. I need to see Natalee coming into that hotel. We ask the Holiday Inn front desk to check on the security videos from Sunday night, May 29, 2005, the night Natalee disappeared, into the morning hours of Monday, May 30. We are told they aren't available. The management is working on getting them for us. About the time we're talking to the people at the front desk about this, we notice Paulus van der Sloot in the lobby. What is he doing here? Looking for security videos perhaps? We also call the Wyndham Hotel and ask to see security footage of their casino on the night Joran's father said he was playing in a poker tournament there. It was the night we arrived on the island. Those tapes are not available right now either.

All the while the tips keep coming in, but there's no sign of Natalee anywhere. It's a sad day. Sadder than yesterday, but probably not as sad as tomorrow will be. Giving the statement leaves me wrung out. Hearing the words of the detective about the drug scheme and how his theory conflicts with what the young men told us in the van der Sloots' front yard is very confusing and deflates my hope. Nothing is adding up. Someone is lying. With no legal or law enforcement support, I am at the mercy of island officials.

Slightly bent over, lips pursed, head low, physically affected by despair, I prepare to say good-bye to Mat, Ruffner, and Jodi, who are leaving today, Wednesday. They have worked so hard and been so courageous. I can't stand to see them go. I feel like I'm melting inside as they say their good-byes. Jug reminds me that soon reinforcements from home will arrive, including my brother Paul and Jug's brother, Jar, and Jug's buddies Bill, Charlie, Mitch, and Jeff. Natalee's father, Dave, and her uncle Phil will also be here tomorrow. Dave wants to focus on ground searches. We've always been able to work together when it comes to our children. This will certainly be the most difficult task we have ever faced, as it would be for any parent. I'll be glad when everyone gets here.

After learning over the past few days that the way to get information is to pay for it, we ask the men who are on their way from home to bring cash. A lot of it. Thousands of dollars are contributed by kind and generous people who want to help. They understand that we will likely have to pay for the clue that will take us to Natalee.

When we tell the new arrivals all that we have learned so far, they'll wish they stayed home.

NEW SIGNS OF HOPE arrive with the new group. They're fresh and enthusiastic and ready to go. We get right to work. They take over the island cell phone Mat was using and start recording tips right away. The first one comes from Alberto the handler. He says that Natalee has been spotted downtown walking around with Wendy and Peter Pan. Can it be true? She has been seen! This is it! But who in the world are these characters, Wendy and Peter Pan? We know better than to question this bizarre tip. The best thing to do is just go follow it. Energy surges as we all anxiously load up and drive toward the cruise ship docks and the nice shopping areas. It's a good way to orient the new group. They can get a look at the island before the night comes and the lead chasing becomes frantic and chaotic.

Toothless, shoeless, and homeless, Wendy is referred to by locals as someone who came to Aruba on vacation several years ago. She got "all cracked up" and stayed. No one really *meets* Wendy. She stays too high, according to the locals. You just see her walking around. We find her all right, walking around like she's in never-never land right in the middle of the major shopping area. She's accompanied by Peter, her island partner. She is scantily dressed, and her sun-damaged skin is visible, making her look much older than she probably is. These two are well-known drug addicts here, and this is the first of several tips that Natalee has been seen with them. We chase down every one of the leads on Wendy and Peter, but none of these ever pans out.

We go back to the hotel to update the new group of men on all that has transpired since we first arrived on the island. They come up with the idea to try to find Joran van der Sloot at his school to see if they can talk with him directly. Bill, Charlie, Mitch, and Jeff head to the International School of Aruba and leave the rest of us at the hotel to continue tracking leads. Upon their arrival, they encounter the assistant headmaster, who takes them to the office. As he leads them, they ask if Joran attends this school. "Yes, yes. And he has been sleeping here." Surprised that he offers this, they store this information and make their way to the office, where the headmaster greets them and invites them in.

"Are you FBI?" the headmaster asks them.

They reply no, that they are friends of the family who are concerned about Natalee's disappearance.

The headmaster shares with them that Paulus and his son Joran visited him yesterday to tell him all the details of what happened. "Paulus and Joran explained that Natalee was dropped off at the Holiday Inn after a trip to the lighthouse. They told me the outside cameras are not working at the hotel," the headmaster says.

How would this father and son already know whether or not the cameras at the hotel were working the night Natalee disappeared? We've been asking for days to see the security footage of the hotel entrance. Perhaps Paulus has too. And why would this father and son go to all the trouble to meet with the school headmaster to offer this detailed story?

The headmaster continues by telling the men from home that Paulus and Joran told him Natalee wanted to go see sharks. The headmaster even makes a suggestion. "Maybe Natalee decided to go swimming and drowned."

With that, one of our men holds up one of Natalee's posters and asks to see Joran. The headmaster declines, saying that because Joran is a minor they cannot see him. Then they ask to speak to Joran's mother, Anita, who is a teacher at the school. The headmaster declines again. Then they ask him if Joran is sleeping at the school. He pauses, then answers, "Yes, Joran slept here last night." Dumbfounded, the four men get up to leave and on their way out attach a poster to the school fence, a poster with the added words *Ask Joran About This Girl.*

It's devastating to hear what took place at the school. We all know what this means. There is something terribly, terribly wrong here. The father and son appear to be campaigning to prove their innocence. The young man the headmaster is calling a minor has special gambling and drinking privileges in the bars and casinos here. He plays blackjack with his father. He's sleeping at his *school.* Paulus van der Sloot already appears to know something about failing cameras at the Holiday Inn. Who are these people, the van der Sloots? Does the father have some kind of political immunity? What are they hiding? We'll find out, and let them know who we are too.

The tips are coming in steadily all day. Natalee has supposedly been at a pizza place, a casino, the beach, a restaurant, a gas station, on the street with Wendy and Peter Pan, and in a Jeep all in one day. But each tip still brings the possibility and the hope that she will be found, so it's encouraging to check out each one. One tip in particular keeps resurfacing—that Jeep. Several callers have reported to us and to the local radio station that Natalee has been seen in a Jeep at a pizza parlor and also at the beach. We can't figure out if there is one Jeep or two. One caller says the driver is known as Theodore. Another says his name is Vader. A well-known drug runner on the island drives a bright yellow Jeep pulling a trailer with a small rubber boat on the back. He reportedly has a lot of cash on him. In the little dinghy is an old oil barrel. This is the most difficult tip for me to listen to so far, as the callers are saying that the barrel in the boat on the back of this Jeep is where Natalee was put so she could be taken out to sea and dumped. It's a horrific thought, and I can't—my mind doesn't want to—comprehend it. We have the tip, but no one can find the jeep, so we have to put it aside for now.

The headline on the posters is changed to KIDNAPPED, because I believe after so much time has passed that this is indeed what has happened. A new batch with the new headline is ready for pickup. The men from home split into two groups to investigate leads and take the van and the rental car. Everyone takes off in a different direction to continue working for Natalee, leaving me at the hotel. So I climb into a cab to go to the print shop. As the driver makes his way, I'm looking out the window and, unbelievably, spot a bright yellow Jeep. It could be the one the callers have described: there's a trailer on the back with a small boat. There's a barrel on the dinghy. It's parked at a pizza restaurant.

I lean from the backseat forward and point a shaking finger, telling the driver frantically, "Over there! Over there! That Jeep. Take me over there!" I ask him whose Jeep it is.

He moans, then sighs with reluctance and answers the question. "It's Vader's Jeep. He very bad. Very bad. He sells drugs for big drug cartel. He's a runner. That's why he has the little boat."

The cabbie explains that the big drug lords have many runners. The runners bring drugs in from the drug boats and vice versa. The cab driver pulls up to the Jeep. Vader, a six-foot-plus, twenty-something young man, is just getting into the driver's side. I roll down my window.

Before I can speak, he sees me and offers, "I'm sorry about Natalee."

That's weird, and his statement takes me aback. I haven't even introduced myself. So I ask him if he knows where she is and explain that there are reports that she has been seen in his vehicle.

He replies, "What about the gray Honda? I thought they were looking into that." And before I can answer he volunteers, "The Coast Guard has already searched my boat."

This is stunning. I never mentioned Deepak's car or this guy's boat. His responses anger me to the core. I feel he has something to hide. He has information on where Natalee is. I just know it. I insist that he come to the Bubali police station and talk to the detective. The cab driver also becomes angry and demands that Vader follow us there. And, surprisingly, he does.

We enter the building where I gave my statement just this morning and ask detective Dennis Jacobs to come out to speak to Vader. The detective asks the young man his name. "Vader" is his answer. I look at Jacobs with eyes that say, "See! See! This is the man! Do something!" Jacobs looks at me and says the reports are that a man named Theodore is the one who has the Jeep we are looking for, not this guy. My mind is spinning as the cab driver and I give up and turn to leave the station. I'm trying to put this together. We get in the cab and drive away.

The Jeep is the most often cited tip we have received so far. How many bright yellow Landcruisers pulling a trailer with a rubber boat and an oil barrel on the back can be driving around this relatively small island? Does Vader have a brother? Or is he one and the same as Theodore? As I look back over my scrappy notes of all the live sightings, it hits me. That's it! I yell to the cabbie to turn around. Turn around! We come back up the road to the police station just as Vader is getting into his Jeep. I run up to his car and reach in the window, pressing my fingers into his upper arm.

"What's your name?" I shout. Three times I ask him, *"What's your name?"*

He doesn't answer. I look in the passenger seat to see Natalee on the front page of the *Diario* newspaper. With the fingers of one hand still pressing into his arm, I reach around with my other hand and open his car door.

"Get out buddy! Get out right now, and get back in that police station!" He knows by my anger that he better comply. I escort Vader by his arm back inside.

"You're hurting me," the young man, half a foot taller than me and twice my size, complains.

"You get in there and tell the detective your real name!" I demand, mad, almost panicked, but contained. Just barely. Jacobs comes out again, and Vader and I replay the same scene that we just did in the parking lot.

"Tell the detective your name! *Tell him!*" I already know the answer. "What is your name?"

And finally the reply comes, sheepishly. "Theodore."

I look at Jacobs, who looks at me.

"See? This is your man. Theodore and Vader are one and the same! Natalee has been seen in this guy's Jeep for the past two days! We have tips on this from the first time the posters went up. You need to talk to this guy! Please! *Do something!*"

Jacobs nods with affirmation and stammers, "I'll talk to him."

No one will ever convince me that the first time I brought Vader/Theodore into the police station this detective didn't know who he was. Everyone knows everyone.

I leave Theodore in the custody of the police. And later we are told that he is related to Joran van der Sloot. They might be cousins. But that's where it ends. He isn't held or searched or interrogated. Nothing comes of our intense and dramatic encounter. It's just one of countless desperate, despicable confrontations we find ourselves in all day and all night long. Searching, probing, pursuing the answer to what happened to Natalee. Answering the calls, following the leads, trusting the tips, and chasing the lies. And so far, nothing.

———————

A NEW STACK OF POSTERS in hand, I return to the Holiday Inn as the men are coming in. Today they searched a small outer island about five hundred yards or so off the shore of Aruba. Tourists go there to snorkel and scuba. The men scoured the rough parts of this place and found little huts. Inside were chairs with ropes and wires around them. "It looks like someone has been, or could be, held captive there," they tell me. "It's really weird. And eerie." They describe seeing drink bottles full of urine inside these huts. "We asked the police if they have searched there. We got the same answer as when we asked them about searching the school where Joran is sleeping. They say they are looking into it ..."

It's late, and we all agree to meet shortly for dinner.

At the restaurant I order a meal, but only eat a bite or two. The others have worked up an appetite, and the meal is a good time for everyone to regroup before the calls start coming in again tonight. As dinner concludes, detective Jacobs appears at our table. He's holding official documents. Surprised to see him here at ten o'clock at night, we invite him to sit down, hoping he has some pertinent information about Natalee. Or answers about the strange clandestine huts. Or reasons why a young man possibly connected with Natalee's disappearance is sleeping at his school. The detective says he just wants me to sign a new statement.

Jug immediately asks him, "What's the difference between this one and the one she gave you this morning?"

Jacobs says that some dates were wrong on that one and have been corrected, and he needs my signature on the new corrected copy.

The document is in Dutch, which is Greek to me. I have no idea what it says. I can't tell if it's different from the one the young officer read to me this morning, which I signed, or not. But all I have to rely on is the Aruban police process, so I gladly submit to his request and sign every single page. Desperate, I will do anything they ask. Maybe I can get a copy of this one. I'll worry about having it translated later. For now, I will trust.

As I hand the papers back to Jacobs, he takes the opportunity to tell the group around the table that he isn't happy about all the running through the drug houses we have been doing.

"But that's where the leads are telling us she is," one of the men says.

"You yourself told me this morning that's where she is, but you guys aren't searching for her," I add.

"You should not disturb our choller houses and our whore-houses," he says. His comment is so incredulous that no one can respond.

We were told that the government flags that fly atop the choller houses signify the places where the drug addicts are allowed to live for free, doing their drugs day in and day out, as long as they don't bother the tourists. But apparently this system isn't working. Aruba may need to rethink its government choller plan. Tourists *are* being bothered. Not to mention possibly robbed and/or held captive, as Jacobs and everyone else on this island have explained to me in the last twenty-four hours.

The table is quiet as Jacobs walks away. We just aren't equipped to respond. We're too shocked that the concern is for the druggies and the whores, not for Natalee. They seem to be more focused on protecting the illegal activities on the island than worrying about the crime victim.

We retire to our rooms by midnight, ready for the onslaught of crazy calls to come, waiting through the night on standby to resume the wild goose chase. We're like dogs chasing their tails. We have no choice but to exhaust every tip, turn over every stone, and follow every lead. No matter how bizarre. No matter how many crack houses we have to search. And it was about to begin.

Wednesday rolls into Thursday when a significant tip comes in at one o'clock from an island newspaper reporter named Julia. She says she has a lead from a local named O.J. that Natalee is definitely being held at a crack house that we have not yet searched. It's on the other side of the island, surrounded by a big wall, as are many of the houses in Aruba. The reporter says we should not tell police or bring any other people. She also instructs us to bring plenty of money and meet her at the Buccaneer restaurant to figure out how to make a deal with the chollers to buy Natalee back. *Buy Natalee back ...*

I put $2,000 in my front pocket and $2,000 in my back pocket. Then Jug and his brother, Jar, and I slip out of the Holiday Inn to follow this lead.

Inside the Buccaneer restaurant the reporter is with her friend, the restaurant owner, and the owner's husband. The tipster, O.J., waits outside in his car while the three of us go inside to map out our strategy. We decide all the men will go to the choller house to see if Natalee is really there. I'm to wait in the restaurant with the two women.

The men leave. Suddenly I'm frightened. It's dark in here. It's about two o'clock in the morning, and everything is shut down. What if the men don't come back? The two women lead me through the darkness to a bar. There's a glass of white wine and a shrimp cocktail on it. "Eat something. Have some wine," they suggest. I put the glass to my lips and take the tiniest taste. I immediately feel it in my head and stop at one sip. I don't want the shrimp. I'm paranoid. Jumpy. A rat startles me as it runs across some exposed beams over the bar. The women tell me to calm down and just relax. Relax? We're trying to buy my daughter back from a drug addict. I'm paralyzed with fear, not sure if I'm actually breathing or not. There isn't much conversation while we wait. What is taking so long?

The restaurant owner asks me if I want to meet her friends. But there's no one here, I think to myself. No one I can *see*. I don't think I want to meet her friends. But the two get up. They motion for me to follow them to the back of the restaurant, where it's darker than midnight. "This is it," I murmur inaudibly. "I'm going to die." There's someone waiting in the back to kill me and take this money. It's all a setup, my exhausted mind concludes. With each slow step in the dark I expect someone to reach out and knock me down, stab me, shoot me, or maybe just abduct me. That's actually a comforting thought. Maybe if they kidnap me, they'll put me wherever Natalee is.

I am very scared. Suddenly the owner flips on the lights and several gigantic aquariums are illuminated all over the restaurant! These are the friends—fish! I don't know if my own mind is playing tricks or if the women know they are scaring me. Either way, it's a relief to see they are only talking about fish. These are the largest sea creatures I have ever seen in domestic captivity. The aquariums are inserted in the walls and the tops of them appear to be open at the back. Probably how the rats get in. For a moment, a very short fraction of a minute, my attention is diverted. Then we hear Jug and Jar walk through the restaurant door, and I run up to the front. They are convinced this is a good lead. So much so that they want to call detective Jacobs and the other men in our group before we all go back to the crack house to get Natalee. This *must* be where she is. My heart is pounding. I'm shaky. We all are. "Please, God, let us find her now."

We place a call to detective Jacobs. He asks us to wait until he gets there to go in. Our friends and the handlers wait with us at the choller house forty-five minutes for the detective, who finally appears walking down an alley next to the house, accompanied by his wife. No other police cars are here. The detective must not have very high hopes for this search. He didn't request any backup. And he brought his wife.

We are all very quiet. We seem to be the only ones on this property. The handlers, Alberto, Claudio, and Eldrith, go around to the back of the house. All the men from home go in the front. The others, including the detective, stand by. The group searches inside and, after a few minutes, comes out. I run to them.

She isn't here. So much anticipation is expended on this search that there isn't a positive ounce of hope left in me. Anger is all there is. And it explodes when I turn to see camera lenses and heads appear one at a time across the top of the wall around the house. The island media are in the bushes, in the trees, all over the place. There's only one way they knew to be here—the reporter. I can't help but feel it was a setup. The media gathered because they thought they would get a shot of Natalee being led out of a crack house. Disheveled. Dirty. Probably incapacitated. I can only imagine the shape she would be in after four days in this situation. This was the image they wanted to show the world.

"You f–kers! Get out of here! Get out of here!" I scream. How dare they try to tarnish her! There's no way I will allow them to see her like this. And photograph her.

It's over. We get in our cars and drive away. Without Natalee.

The Stations

Cursing is my only outlet. My only method of venting. Until last night I managed to do it in private. Letting loose and expelling the anger and frustration that's eating me alive, I use the worst words I can think of. I haven't ever cussed before the way I have in the past few days. It comes out of me after midnight when the feelings of despair overwhelm me. And when exhaustion takes hold. This time is no different, as we drive back to the Holiday Inn. The day started with the statement at the Bubali police station. It ends with another busted lead. The days and nights blend together as opportunities to get help appear and dissipate as fast as the hope of finding Natalee. I know I can get to the bottom of what has happened to her. There are so many "live sightings." Alberto told us on Monday when he first brought us to the hotel from the airport that "everyone knows everyone here." I cling to the theory that someone must know something.

Jug and I are in the hotel room only a few minutes when there is a knock at the door. A hotel employee says they have the video footage of the lobby from the night Natalee disappeared ready for me to look at downstairs. Immediately a second wind comes with this four o'clock news. We rush downstairs to a small room near the main front desk. There's no sign on the door; very nondescript. We're advised to go inside. Slowly I open the door. As it widens, the opening reveals police officials, one after the other after the other, a dozen or more of them standing around in this small room. At four o'clock in the morning. Waiting for us. There's a desk and a computer screen. It's the security room. I don't know what is behind the partition that cuts the room in half, making it small.

Seeing all these officers makes me think maybe they know something. As I sit down to watch the tapes, a hotel employee hands me the records I've been asking for showing the key entries to Natalee's room on May 30. Three keys were used. Three of the four girls entered the room. One did not. I was afraid of that. The black-and-white footage plays. Suddenly a girl with light hair crosses the threshold of the lobby. The video is grainy, but clearly shows the lobby entrance of the Holiday Inn. I ask them to rewind it and play it again. I recognize her. I want it to be Natalee, but know it's not. It's Mat's daughter. I ask to see it again. Again. Again. Play it once more. Now again. More than ten times they rewind the spot on the tape that shows this young woman coming into the hotel and stopping at the front desk to get a key.

I so want it to be my daughter. Maybe if I look at it enough times I can make it her. Please! Play it again. Slow it down. Now pause it. Please, be Natalee. But it isn't. I already know the second time I see it that it isn't her. The tapes play out.

The night passes, and Natalee never appears at the hotel where Joran and Deepak so elaborately demonstrated they left her. She never came back. She never got out of that car and stumbled and bumped her head like they told me. She got into Deepak's car at Carlos 'n Charlie's, but they didn't bring her here like they said they did. And I surmise that this must be why Paulus is telling people, like the headmaster, that the outside hotel cameras are broken. So no one would find out the truth.

———

THERE IS SILENCE in the little crowded room. Eventually the quiet is broken as police officers and detectives who witness the same evidence we do in the wee hours of Thursday morning begin to speak very softly, almost whispering to one another in Dutch and Papiamento. I don't know what they're saying, but they are very subdued.

They all see for themselves that Joran, Deepak, and Satish never brought Natalee back to the Holiday Inn. Those three made everything up, from how they took her to the lighthouse to see sharks to how they left her at the hotel. Joran isn't a tourist, and he isn't staying at the Holiday Inn. He isn't nineteen years old, as he told Natalee's friends. He's seventeen. It's all lies. All of it. The dialog between Natalee and Joran, the places they went, how they got home—concocted. And for what reason? Surely to cover the truth about what has really happened to Natalee. They know. And now we all know they lied. But what they *don't* know is that I'm willing to wait out all their lies to get to the truth. I have the rest of my life to find out what has happened to Natalee.

Descending to the lowest place the human spirit can fall, I am physically and mentally weak. Barely able to get back to Natalee's hotel room. Feet dragging. Posture stooping. My soul is barren. Empty. I try to walk, but I'm spinning. My mind cannot comprehend what we just saw. It's sickening to think what they have done with her. To her. It's disgusting to think of the evidence that has been lost in the past four days. I personally handed over the two young men and the car she was seen getting into to island authorities. They have seen the video now, the proof that the three locals haven't told us the truth about where they took her. My work is finished. It's up to the police to take it from here. They now have the information they need to go get these young men and do what should have been done the very first night we encountered them in the van der Sloots' front yard. The car should have been searched and impounded. A search warrant should have allowed the police to go inside that house. Joran and Deepak should have been detained, interrogated. *Now* surely the police will take the actions that should have been taken days ago.

––––––––––

NATALEE'S PURPLE DUFFEL BAG is on her bed. Out loud I tell her I'm sorry. I tell her how hard we have tried. How hard we have worked to find her. Suddenly it feels like I may not be able to take another breath. Or another step. How much can a person take before completely imploding? The tough exterior is wearing thin. The mental strength that's part of who I am, that "suck it up and press on" upbringing, is not enough to keep me afloat any longer. It lasted four days. It held me up when I needed it most. But now I need serious help. I am caving in. And I know what I need to do.

It must be at least ninety degrees at this predawn hour, but I put on one of Jug's jackets anyway to hide the four-day-old body odor. Taking one of the KIDNAPPED posters with me, I leave him in the room to go find a cab. The bellman waves one down. I get in and tell the driver to take me to a church. The driver says, "Non, non. No churches open now." He is uncooperative and unwilling. He says he doesn't know where any are. The bellman offers to find me another ride and summons a second cab. I get in and make the same request. "Take me to a church or a chapel or somewhere I can pray."

The foundation of my faith is built on the teachings of Jesus Christ. God is ever present. Ritual is unnecessary to call on Him, who already knows my suffering. But today is different. I have prayed constantly, but I feel the need to pray harder. Louder. Get to God. Hasn't He heard me?

This driver knows where to go. We leave the resort area and get into the island's interior, which has become all too familiar in the past few days as we searched and searched for Natalee. Passing shacks and pitifully disadvantaged neighborhoods. Skinny stray dogs in the streets. Donkeys tied to stumps in the front of houses. There are very few lights in these homes. The driver curves around the road to a point where he turns left. He makes another turn or two, and what little civilization there is disappears. I'm not sure what is going to happen. And I don't care. It doesn't matter. Nothing matters.

He slows down and pulls over, finally stopping. He tells me to get out. So I do. He points to the side of the road, past the giant cacti, and tells me to walk in that direction. So I do, and I come upon a beautiful white cross. I look up beyond it to see a long row of crosses leading up the hillside. The driver motions me toward the first one, and I stumble to it, clutching the poster.

At the cross I fall to my knees and cry out to God. "Please! Give her back to me! Let me have her back!" I take pebbles from the ground and rub them across her picture. Praying. Crying. Begging. And I begin to feel. Deeply. After being numb for days there is now pain. Torturous pain. Anguish. I get up and move to the next cross. I get down on my knees again and ask God again, "Please help me. Tell me what to do. Tell me how to get her back." I pray. Pleading with Him.

I rise and make my way up the hillside to the next cross and the next one and the next, repeating my prayers. I hear the faint crackling sounds of the cab as it rolls along. Two wheels on the pavement and two off the side in the gravel. The driver keeps a respectful distance, letting me pray, letting me grieve. I am looking to the sky, which is growing bluer as dawn breaks, and talking to God. And as I reach the fifth cross, the answer to these prayers comes. Complete peace blankets me, and I am still. It's a familiar feeling, yet unknown to me like this before now.

It comes in total stillness. Silence. And in this instant I know that Natalee is with God.

I understand that from the moment she got into Deepak Kalpoe's car her heavenly Father wrapped His loving arms around her and cared for her through whatever ordeal she encountered that night. I don't know if she is alive or not, but I know that He is with her.

He entrusted me with her care for eighteen years. Now I must trust Him to care for her. So I never ask Him why. Why Natalee? Why me? I don't ask. To do that undermines faith. Instead, I form an "acceptance trust" with Him there on the windy hillside. God never questioned me when she was in my care. I must not question Him. I realize that He is as proud of her as I am. Thoughts of Natalee's personal relationship with God come to me. He knows her very well. And she knows Him.

Natalee was very active in the Community Ministry for Girls in Mountain Brook all four years throughout high school. The founder and director, Donna Greene, shared a special moment with me just before graduation. A few months earlier Natalee came to Donna on several occasions and asked her to pray for certain things for her. Donna told Natalee that her own prayers are heard by God just as much and encouraged her to give Him a chance to make Himself known to her. Following the very last Bible group meeting about two weeks or so ago, Natalee told her friends to go on without her. She hung back for twenty or thirty minutes to talk to Donna. She was excited and glowing as she told Donna that she knew for certain that she had communicated with God, that He had moved on her behalf. She knew He heard her. Donna had never seen her like this and was delighted to witness the connection Natalee had made. Donna's first words of support when Natalee went missing were, "She knows how to call on God." In these thoughts I receive the blessed assurance from the Creator that rescues me. And I am at peace.

It has been a deliberate and diligent task to keep my mind intact for the past four days, shunning emotions to the best of my ability. Now it's time to release this control. It's time to feel with the heart what the mind is incapable of comprehending. I am keenly aware of the moment that my mind and heart separate from one another, as the burden of the world that has been riding specifically and squarely on my left shoulder is literally lifted. There is instant relief. The weight is gone. I move to the next cross, making my way on up the hill stopping and praying at all fourteen crosses. The Stations of the Cross. The depiction of the walk Jesus made to His crucifixion.

The sun is up as I reach the top of the hill to see the Alto Vista chapel. When I step onto the chapel grounds I am free, liberated from the pain for a precious few moments. The police have their suspects. I can lay down my sword. The wind is blowing hard, and I feel Natalee. I talk to her. Promise to find her. Get justice for her. And pledge never to give up. Never.

Inside the open chapel are candles lined up on both sides of an altar. The majority of the population in Aruba is Roman Catholic, and numerous rosary beads hang on the walls. Little crosses and other mementos decorate the small dark candlelit room where a few wooden pews lead to the altar. The cab driver comes inside with me. The Arubans are very religious, very spiritual people. He prays with me. I light a candle for Natalee. The driver leaves me alone, and I stay here for a very long time before getting back in the car. He patiently waits for me. I will come back here later today and every day, I decide.

The driver takes me back to the hotel. I think about what just happened, pondering the human spirit. Apparently it can withstand a lot more than I ever dreamed possible. Mom is right: God is good. All my life I've heard people of many faiths talk about "taking it to the cross and turning it over to the Lord" or just simply "turning it over." I suppose that's what just happened to me. I turned it over. Not the work that has to be done. Just the burden. I cast it upon Him so that I may be sustained. And I am renewed, resilient. Thankful for however long this resurgence in energy will carry me. I will pick up one foot and put it down. Then the other one will follow. I will breathe. There is much to be done.

———

AFTER THIS THREE-HOUR PILGRIMAGE I return to the hotel lobby to find Jug, who with very little rest is dressed and ready to start another tumultuous, demanding, and draining day. He meets me at the front entrance. The moment he looks at me he says, "You seem different."

Looking at him, I reply, "I am."

And with that I go to Natalee's hotel room. The bedside lamp stays on around the clock and spotlights her beautiful portrait. Removing the clothes that I've been wearing since Marilyn, Linda, and I left Memphis four days ago, I take a bath, put on clean clothes, eat a few bites of fruit, then call Marilyn. "Would you do something for me?" I ask her. "Please go to my house and unpack Natalee's *Wizard of Oz* set. You know ... the one we

bought for each of our daughters. Then I need you to take Dorothy's little house from your daughter's set and put it with Natalee's set. It will make me feel better." I know it's weird. I'm not
a superstitious person. But it's bugging me that I didn't buy the
little house for Natalee's set. And I can't help but feel that if the
missing piece is in place then maybe things will somehow be
"right" again. Complete. Marilyn doesn't hesitate and agrees to
do this right away. Relieved, I head back to the lobby where
plans are being made for a huge land search. One week ago
today I saw Natalee disappear into the beam of light at the front
door of her friend's house. Maybe Thursday is our lucky day.
Maybe today we'll find her.

A Cord of Three

"This is Beth. Tell me wha'cha got."

There's no time for chit-chat on the island cell phone, which is the tip line. I want to get to every caller without missing one. Just in case it's "the" one. This phone, Natalee's cell phone, and my cell are on me at all times. Natalee's remains silent, but the other two keep ringing. Reporters want interviews. Islanders and people from home offer their support. It's as if more than one hundred families in Birmingham—the parents of the other students on the trip—have lost a child. And they're taking action the best way they know how. Governor Bob Riley, Senator Richard Shelby, Congressman Spencer Bachus, and a host of other Alabama political leaders have been swamped all week with requests for State Department assistance from their constituents who want to help Natalee. This unity from home gives us great motivation.

Right now it's Dave calling from the site where the Royal Dutch Marines are organizing for a land search. The Aruba

Search and Rescue Team, the Aruban Red Cross, members of the International Friends of Aruba organization, Aruba Child Protective Services, and other volunteers offer their assistance as the week progresses. Remarkable things happen when people stand by one another. Optimism flourishes. Spirits are fed. There is strength in unity, and that strength creates energy for the people who are hurting.

The energy is felt all the way from home, where I'm told Mountain Brook is painted yellow with bows. Every storefront, mailbox, front door, and fence. Even bows as hood ornaments on cars declare: "We are missing a loved one." Beautiful yellow bows seem so innocent, soft in the way the ribbons fold over each other, delicate with long hanging strands that turn in the breeze. But sad for the pain they represent. Someone who should be at home isn't. The bows say it all. Smith's Variety store and Norton's Florist in Mountain Brook are running out of yellow ribbon because so many people want to show their love for Natalee; be part of her team. With these bows and the mounting support from the community, neighbors we know and those we have never met begin to share our sadness and pain. And express theirs. Empathy gives us more strength.

Mountain Brook Community Church, where daily prayer services are being held for Natalee, is fast becoming command central for everyone to lend support to one another. I worry about the other students who were on the trip. The FBI is questioning them. The media want interviews with them. It must be terribly unnerving. Most senior classes have dispersed for the summer, many for life. But Natalee's friends remain together, loyal, steadfast in their vigil, waiting for her to come home. Reverend Kallam and his staff are giving them a place of solace and activities, so they can actually do something for their missing friend. The prayer bracelets they work on every day at the church are made of three cords of colorful yarn braided together to represent Ecclesiastes 4:12:

> Though one may be overpowered, two can defend themselves. A cord of three strands is not quickly broken.

Indeed. Natalee was one overpowered. The three cords that will not be quickly broken are faith, hope, and unity.

Everything evolves very quickly in the first couple of days. The outreach movement expands rapidly as people from the nearby community of Gardendale, led by a big-hearted man named Eddie, construct a giant Wall of Hope at the church where messages and prayers are left for Natalee. This becomes the backdrop for press conferences facilitated by my friend Sunny and my sister-in-law Marcia, who is in public relations. Between them they have fifty years of media experience. Marcia is representing the family in front of the camera, and Sunny works behind it.

Carla is an American who works for the New York agency that handles Aruba's tourism publicity. She evolves into a media coordinator for us here, helping to field interview requests and other matters on the island. She becomes our on-camera family spokesperson on the island, Marcia's counterpart.

The national and international media are beginning to pick up Natalee's story as reporters and producers migrate from Birmingham to the island. FOX, CNN, NBC, CBS, ABC, BBC,

AP. Everybody. Natalee has an army of hope behind her with the prayers and support from her hometown, the news media, and the islanders. Maybe all this attention will bring out the answer. I'm pumped up in my fresh, clean yellow shirt today. This is my bow. My symbol of hope.

The Holiday Inn becomes the focus of a flurry of media activity toward the end of the first week following Natalee's disappearance. Microphones are set up on a podium in a large meeting room designated as the press room. Production assistants untangle long cords and lay them out across the floor to connect the mics to the cameras. Sitting atop tall tripods the large, round, black lenses of these cameras are aimed in one direction, lined up like the Dutch marines along the beach. People on cell phones, taking notes, calling out to one another create an awkward level of excitement.

Representatives and senators I've never heard of from many states are reaching out to us by phone and e-mail. We're told that someone from the office of the U.S. Secretary of State contacted officials in Aruba for an update on the situation here. Political and business leaders with experience in international relations clearly understand the complexity of this situation and the potential for problems such as corruption much more than we do.

It must nauseate them to hear an Aruban government spokesman state on the *O'Reilly Factor* that Aruba doesn't have a drug problem. "That's only good for the movies," he says.

In fact, the United States is working hard to help combat the drug traffic in the Caribbean. And no wonder. We've seen the drug houses, the chollers. It's a very serious problem here. "Don't

KIDNAPPED

**LAST SEEN AT CARLOS & CHARLIES
MONDAY, MAY 29, 2005 1:30AM
NATALEE HOLLOWAY
CAUCASIAN AMERICAN FEMALE
BLUE EYES / LONG BLOND HAIR
5'4" 110 LBS.   18 YEARS OLD**

ANY INFORMATION
PLEASE CALL 587-6222
OR CALL POLICE STATION 100

This is the poster we immediately plastered all over Aruba.

Now, all new tips about my daughter's disappearance can be phoned in directly to a special FBI hotline number: (205) 326-6166.

Thank you.

Please help us search
lets meet at 10am at t'

Family of teen missing in Aruba

als: Hunt may become criminal probe

By HANNAH WOLFSON
News staff writer

Police in Aruba said Friday the prognosis was growing darker as the search for a missing Mountain Brook teen dragged on.

Natalee Holloway disappeared early Monday on a senior class trip to the Caribbean island. On day five of the search, it she is not found by Sunday, the case could become a criminal investigation, said Jules Sambo, a superintendent for the Aruba police.

"As the days pass and we know nothing about her ... we probably can start to

think about something more serious," he said.

Holloway's family posted fliers blaring the word "KIDNAPPED" in red, but police said they had no evidence to support such a claim.

Holloway's aunt, Marcia Twitty, said the family changed the fliers' heading from "missing" to dramatize the urgency of their search.

"They're getting tired and they want answers," she said "We've got to find her."

▶ See Missing, Page 7A

Teen's disappearance raises concerns over

By KATHY SEALE
News staff writer

Patrick Veigl won't graduate from Hewitt-Trussville High School until 2007. Nevertheless, his father Dennis Veigl spent part of friday discussing senior trips with his colleagues at Honours Golf Co.

The disappearance this week of Natalee

Ann Holloway, the Mountain Brook teen on a senior trip to Aruba, brought home what can happen when your child's away from home.

"It's sure heightened awareness," Dennis Veigl said.

And it has folks all over the Birmingham area talking about the safety of senior trips, which nearly always are orga-

nized by parents and not sanc the schools.

Kristy Duke said Holloway's disappearance made her stop and think whether she'll allow her children, w tend Erwin High School, to lea country for a senior trip.

▶ See Trips, Page

Search grows more urge
for teen missing in A

Thousands comb Aruba
in search for missing teen

By HANNAH WOLFSON
News staff writer

ORANGESTAD, Aruba — An estimated 2,500 Aruban residents turned out Monday to help look for Natalee Holloway, 18, of Mountain Brook, but the broadened search turned up nothing.

The Aruban government called on all citizens to aid in the search, and it released about 4,000 government workers at lunchtime to encourage them to join in.

Holloway's mother, Beth Twi she can barely handle the burd many people's concern.

"It's hard to comprehend th outpouring of support," she s picked at her food in a local taurant, where the maitre d' with a hug and her waiter daughter would be found.

▶ See A

NEWS

prosecutions still a priority / 5B

Metro briefs
Crime reports
Weather

al.com   *www.al.com*

SING IN ARUBA

Holloway's mom returning to islar

itty leaves today, plans to y another month

NNAH WOLFSON
staff writer

o months into the search for her iter in Aruba, Beth Twitty didn't want even a few days off to come back to ma.

, after three days at home in Mountain k, Twitty said she's returning to Aruba "ready to fight," and she'll be carrying cial piece of cargo: photos of the yellow ns that line the streets of Natalee Holy's hometown.

want to take them with me so I can look em and I can also show Aruba," Twitty as she drove around running errands

Monday. "I can't think of anything better to take."

Twitty flew home Saturday to spend time with her 16-year-old son, Matt, with other family, and with friends of her daughter. Holloway, 18, disappeared May 30 while on a graduation trip to Aruba.

Her mother said her family's home feels empty without her daughter.

"I don't want to be there," she said. "I'm ready to go get her."

Twitty left her clothes and papers in her room at Aruba's Wyndham Hotel, where she plans to stay another month. One of her tasks during her short trip home was to arrange a leave with the Mountain Brook school system, where she works as a speech pathologist.

She took care of a few everyday tasks, including a dental appointment and taking the

family dog, Macy, to the vet for her summer haircut. The pastor who had married her and her husband, George "Jug" Twitty, prayed with them at home.

Twitty also went twice to the prayer wall set up for her daughter at Mountain Brook Community Church. She first stopped at midnight Saturday, soon after arriving in town. She returned Sunday with a group of Holloway's girlfriends, including those who plan to attend the University of Alabama with her this fall. Twitty said the university understands that "everything's on hold right now."

She said the trips to the wall reassured her because she feared the good wishes she has received from around the world were only for her and not her daughter.

▶ See **Missing**, Page **5B**

Beth Twitty

June 11, 2005

M 3

'Something bad happened' to Hollow

Family conti

Three Men to Appear Before Aruban Judge

er is alive

chaperones celebrating their graduation from Mountain Brook High School.

lative said her family contin-
he is alive. Rumors
he is dead

Oduber asked the pres ports that one of th held in the case had c us do our jobs in a de he said.

Carla Caccavale, a for the family, said:
their way to recove
ers from

MISSING

mother faithful, but ready for worst

cape. Inside the tiny church, she lit a candle for her daughter, then knelt to pray.

"I have complete trust and faith in God, that he is taking care of Natalee," she said. "I believe that he will deliver Natalee to me, and I believe there will be a resolution to this."

Twitty, 44, said Sunday she believes three young men who were with her daughter the day she vanished know what happened to her, and Aruban authorities should pressure them to reveal the information.

She also said she thought that two former hotel security guards detained in her daughter's disappearance are innocent and

"All three of those boys know what happened to her," Twitty told the Associated Press. "They all know what they did with her that night."

Holloway disappeared May 30, just a few hours before she was to return home from the trip to Aruba with 124 recent Mountain Brook High School graduates.

Five suspects are being held in the case. The two former security guards, Abraham Jones, 28, and Antonius Mickey John, 30, will appear before a judge sometime in the next three days to determine whether they will stay in jail.

Aruba — The Holloway, the teen who has ere for two day that her ws her to be orst.

ned crowds of who prayed o her daugh-

rime minister ross the island weekend serv-

ndful of close sited the his-anpel perched

Beth Twitty, mother of Natalee Holloway, lights a candle Sunday in Alto Vista chapel.

Our early years before the divorce. Natalee, her younger brother, Matt, and her father, Dave Holloway.

Natalee always loved the
outdoors, especially the beach.

Such a
personality!
Natalee
learned to
dance at an
early age and
loved it, and
she always had
great friends.

A girl's best friends. Natalee with her adoring brother, Matt, and her much-beloved collie, Macy, whose presence comforts me to this day.

Natalee, an amazing young woman, almost all grown up. These photos represent her high school years. Such a talent, such a beauty. She wore the same prom dress two years in a row because she liked it so much. *(Opposite)*: My daughter was so happy on her graduation day with her honor cords and her proud Mom and Grandma . . . just days before she flew to Aruba with her friends and tragically vanished from our lives.

If you could have any superhuman power, what would it be? Why?

9-11-03

If I had any superhuman power, it would be to predict the future. Sometimes I have a really tough time making decisions because I don't know what the results will be in the future. I wish I had the ability to predict the future so that I would know how decisions I make affect me. For example, I want to know what type of job I will hold in the future so that I know which college and what courses will be the best for me. I also would like to know when I get married, how many children I will have, and where I will live. The superhuman power of predicting the future would definitely be the best power for me to have.

(Above): It saddens me to read this journal entry written by Natalee as a class assignment where she predicts her life. *(Opposite):* Our nightmare begins. I flew to Aruba the minute I heard the news that she was missing, and for months I stayed on the island with volunteers, as did Natalee's stepfather, George "Jug" Twitty, who joined me in Aruba as well as at a press conference in Alabama with the state's governor, Bob Riley, as he signed the boycott.

(*Above*): Joran van der Sloot.
(*Left*): Anita and Paul van der Sloot.
(*Below, left*): Deepak Kalpoe.
(*Below, right*): Satish Kalpoe.

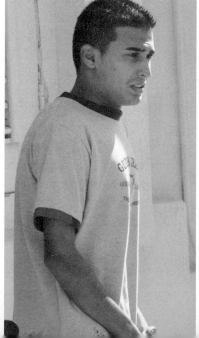

(*Above*): I found my spiritual footing when a wonderful Aruban taxi driver took me to this inspirational place where I "walked" the Stations of the Cross and prayed for God's mercy and guidance. (*Right*): At a prayer vigil at the Emmanuel Church in Oranjestad, Aruba two weeks after Natalee's disappearance. (*Below*): Alone in my hotel room in Palm Beach, Aruba, surrounded by messages, letters, and gifts of sympathy sent from all around the world.

(*Opposite*): We never gave up. Messages and crosses for my missing daughter decorate a memorial "wall of hope" in our hometown of Mountain Brook, Alabama, where many of her friends gathered regularly to make "prayer bracelets" to keep hope alive. (*Above*): Tourists in Aruba also shared their prayers. Two years later, I am still without my daughter, but never without her spirit. (*Below*): Reading letters in the Wyndham Hotel room, studying messages left for Natalee at the Wall of Hope, and finding solace as I often did in the thousands of notes of love, prayer, and support. Even now, in my new home starting a new life, I still receive messages from around the world.

(Above): In my new home in Birmingham, Alabama, I have Natalee's beautiful daybed in my office, where this photo was taken this summer as I read her high school "journal." *(Right):* To my knowledge, this is the last photo taken of Natalee before she disappeared in Aruba. It was taken just before she and her friends went to the popular tourist spot Carlos 'n Charlie's.

give up. Stay the course. Keep the pressure on," Senator Trent Lott tells me. "We see them dragging you through hell down there," Senator Richard Shelby says. They know that if we were at home and Natalee went missing, we could call on our local police and sheriffs and get help. Not here.

"Hold on, Natalee. Just hold on," I tell her. "We're trying so hard." Can she see us? Does she know how hard we're working? Is she in a place that has TV or newspapers? I hope so. I want her to know. So she will stay strong, just as I am trying to do. "Stay strong," Natalee, "until we can get there."

Between the well-wishers and the media people who stop me I can hardly move through the hotel lobby now. The vice-consul from the U.S. Consulate General office on the neighboring island of Curaçao is on her way. Support is growing. And we are overwhelmed and uplifted. But it is all so very surreal.

We still want to get help from the FBI, and we learn that protocol requires that Aruba officially "invite" the Bureau to come here to help out. So we hold a special press conference to broadcast a plea to Aruba to invite the FBI to assist. The response is yes! The FBI is going to be invited to work alongside the Aruban investigators. And we are very relieved to learn that FBI legal attaché Doug Shipley is on his way here to help us. Another press statement is made in which we profusely thank the Arubans for inviting the FBI in.

Reporters and producers want information about Natalee. They want to know all about her, see more. That means going into her duffel bag and looking for her camera. I haven't been able to do that yet. Actually open it up and look at her clothes.

See her things packed there. But now I need to. Now is the opportunity to get her picture broadcast worldwide in the hope that someone has seen her.

As I slowly unzip the bag, her camera reveals itself right on top. Without disturbing the other contents, I remove the camera card and carry it downstairs where a local magazine writer and an AP reporter are waiting. The writer has a laptop and downloads the photos. With one eye closed I can only glance at the screen in short intervals. It's unbearable to see these.

It's graduation night. Natalee is standing with her dad. She and her college roommate-to-be are in our front yard in their white caps and gowns. And then a photo of our faces close together after the ceremony reveals itself. That was her night. She had made it! So much promise. She wore her honors cords so proudly. And looked so happy, so grown up. It was only a week and a half ago that these pictures were taken, but it feels like months. When I was at the lake with my family last week, they all asked me to send them graduation pictures. No one ever could have imagined that the way they would get to see Natalee in her cap and gown was in the news.

I'm seeing these pictures for the first time. And soon the world will see them too.

————————

CONCERNED FRIENDS BACK HOME rally to form teams of helpers to come relieve those who are already here. Delta Airlines flight attendants offer their buddy passes. U.S. Airways agrees to lock in the lowest fare for anyone traveling to Aruba to help us. And they assign a special customer service representative to our case.

Her name is Nancy, and she lovingly and patiently handles all of our numerous requests and schedule changes. A neighbor buys plane tickets for three teacher friends, Carol, Sue, and Martee, to come help me. They arrive on the island Friday afternoon. After a brief tearful greeting, they hand over a big bag of beautiful prayer cards and bracelets made by Natalee's friends. About the size of a driver's license, the cards have Natalee's picture and Ecclesiastes 4:12 printed on them. "We'll use these to meet people," I tell them.

Part of the daily work is to hit the streets to talk to people. Make eye contact. Ask questions. Introduce myself as Natalee's mom. If Alberto the handler is right and "everyone knows everyone" in Aruba, then someone knows something about what happened to Natalee. The prayer cards and bracelets are an excellent vehicle to help us open communications with people.

I immediately give the three women assignments. "Sue, can you handle the media calls? They all want interviews, and we need to figure out how to manage that. Work with Carla. She's our media person here. Carol, can you follow up with the high school and get a copy of Natalee's transcript? We want to establish her character in the media. Getting her records won't be easy because school is out. Martee, I need you to help me with the posters. Mom is giving $10,000 for a reward, and we need to make new posters." The women receive on-the-job training.

By Friday night we're a well-oiled machine in three groups. Jug and the men from home search all night and try to get a little rest in the daytime, but theirs is pretty much a round-the-clock operation. Natalee's father, Dave, and his brother, Phil, facilitate land searches all day with other volunteers. And the women focus on meeting people and hanging posters. Then all three groups converge in the hotel lobby in the evenings.

Dave's group is always rough and scratched up after traipsing through thorny brush and cacti. The women are sweaty and tired. And Jug's group is just getting ready for the night. They will continue their searches, expecting to see Natalee's face around the next corner or behind the next door. Putting themselves in harm's way. Many of the crack-house and whorehouse proprietors they have encountered were armed. One of our men had a gun put to his head last night.

We often ask to meet with police. But they don't always show up. And if they do, they usually don't have any information. Or at least say they don't. The FBI isn't privy to much, but at least FBI legal attaché Doug Shipley is here now. So when the groups converge in the afternoon, the family has a daily FBI briefing in an empty hotel room designated as the "007 room." Then we get back with the others to discuss our findings and prepare for the nightly TV interviews followed by the tips.

We learn "media rules" by necessity very, very quickly. And I understand what it means to have a double-edged sword. I want to accommodate everyone. They may have the power to find Natalee, but the requests are out of control. Carla and Sue are working full-time to schedule the interviews here. Marcia and Sunny are doing the same in Birmingham. *Once you open this gate, you can't close it.*

The island is no more equipped to handle the "media tsunami" than we are. And the authorities are not happy with all the attention. For us, the support is great, but difficult to manage. We're not sure of the impact all these news reports are having, because we can't see most of these shows here. CNN is all we get in our hotel room. But if we're getting CNN, then so is the rest of the island, and we're encouraged by that.

The news shows keep asking to talk to us, so we keep obliging. We have to be told where to look, how to sit, when to listen, when to speak. We've never done any of this before. My only experience was in the few island interviews I did with local media the other day. Doing the interviews is not scary, because I'm so driven to find Natalee that the lights and cameras and people aren't intimidating at all. It's just that we aren't sure what to do. But the media representatives are helpful, understanding. Everyone from the morning shows like *Today, Good Morning America,* and the *CBS Early Show,* to name a few, as well as the evening cable shows the *O'Reilly Factor, On the Record with Greta Van Susteren, Nancy Grace, Larry King Live, Hannity & Colmes,* and many others want to know about Natalee. By the time tonight's live shots and interviews are broadcast, the reward climbs from $10,000 to $50,000, thanks to contributions from home and from businesses on the island. Fifty thousand dollars is almost twice as many Aruban dollars, called florins. Surely for close to 100,000 florins someone will talk. Surely.

Doing our interviews in the same room or on the same balcony as the Aruban officials who are also being interviewed is a good way for us to get information. We hear what they are saying on TV. We hear the promises they are making. A government spokesman says in an interview that he is working closely with me and is making me available to the media. I'm quite surprised to hear this, because I have never met this man. A police official actually says in one TV interview that there should be an answer in Natalee's case in a few days. If this is true, maybe the reward is making a difference.

We retire around two in the morning before Saturday morning's first interview, a "phoner" with an American national network at five. Sue brings me the phone, and I do the interview flat on my back in the bed.

"Beth, how much sleep have you had?" she wants to know.

"Since Monday through last night ... uh ... nine hours," I calculate.

The three women are concerned about this, but soon realize that lack of sleep is less of a conscious decision to self-deprive now than a necessity. Sleep is simply hard to come by because of the tips that start right after midnight and continue throughout the night.

In fact, since entrusting Natalee's care to God, I welcome sleep when I can get it. Nothing in my dreams is worse than my waking hours. Ironically, sleep takes me *out* of the nightmare. No question though, the lack of sleep is having an effect. After holding it together all day, in front of others and in front of TV cameras, night is when emotions spiral out of control.

Feeling was unleashed at the cross, and it is a being of its own. It can soothe me, and it can torment me. It empowers me. Yet I throw things when I'm alone in the room. Shoes. Apples from a fruit basket. Whatever is within reach when the urge strikes. Sometimes the crying is inconsolable, and I hug the purple duffel bag. Over and over. I just hug it.

When Jug and I are in Natalee's room by ourselves, we kneel and pray together for her, staring at her picture on the bedside table. Where we keep the light on. Just like all parents do when they're waiting for their children to come home.

Another day passes. And tomorrow and the next day and the next we'll put on our game faces and do it all over again until we find her.

———

"IT'S LIKE THAT MOVIE *Groundhog Day*," I tell Carol, Sue, and Martee. "Same thing every day. Take the calls. Check out the tips. Search. Put up posters. Talk to people. Do interviews." Being special education teachers like me, they completely understand the drill. Keep chipping away. Don't give up.

I want to show them all the places Natalee has been spotted so far. We take a cab all the way to the other end of the island, to the undesirable town of San Nicolas, the lower socioeconomic area, where an oil refinery is located. The women are astounded to see people standing on the street smoking crack. Out in the open. In front of children. They're even more shocked when I suggest we stop and get out to talk to the people. In San Nicolas they want money to put up reward posters, but nonetheless they all know about Natalee. And I believe they care about her. There is anger here about the situation. They want attention turned to Joran van der Sloot, just as we do. But if the theory is true that drug addicts have her, this is just as good a place as any to hang posters.

Soon our mission is interrupted with a call from the media.

"Do you know what's going on at the Allegro?"

We don't. And our first lesson in the speed of media is under way. It's very possible a reporter may have the news of Natalee before we do. And broadcast it. This time a thoughtful NBC producer gives us a heads-up. He calls the family in Birmingham and suggests they "call the family in Aruba right away. Something is not good." It's a crazy circle of calls. Police are searching the Allegro, a resort hotel under renovation a few buildings down from the Holiday Inn. Jug finds out about it after the media and police are already swarming the property. And he doesn't want me to come to the Allegro. He gives me updates by cell phone every few minutes as the searchers go room to room. They're acting on a tip that there's blood. And a body. Jug is beside himself. And I'm the very last one to find out what is going on.

The rest of the world might very well find out what happened to Natalee before we do. Whatever the news is, this is not how I want my mom to hear it. But she hears this and calls me, sobbing. Back in Arkansas, she is glued to the TV waiting for any word of her beautiful granddaughter. And today the headlines tell her that searchers are looking for a body in a vacant hotel. And it could be Natalee's.

It breaks my heart to think of her there, so far away. Not knowing. Scared for me here. Worried sick. "Mom, y'know, we don't know for sure if Natalee is in there. I know it looks bad. But we don't know, Mom, we just don't know. We have to wait and see." When I talk to her it's usually to diffuse the rumors.

"You know I will call you, Mom. You will hear it from me. No one else." She calms down.

And after hours of searching, there's no body in the Allegro. Nothing. Just another false alarm.

For Carol, Sue, and Martee, orientation is complete. And just in time before the nightly tips begin.

"This is Beth. Tell me wha'cha got."

It's the police spokesman calling the tip line. "We have a girl, and we think she is Natalee. Go to Bubali station. We want you to identify her."

About this time Jug, who is out on searches, gets the same tip from the island newspaper reporter. "Julia found a girl and thinks it's Natalee. Let's meet at Bubali."

The three women and I run to a cab. "Take us to Bubali station. Please! Hurry!"

Emotions swing into a high-pitched whirl of anticipation. But on the way something doesn't feel right. I've been to this station several times now. We seem to be going the wrong way. Sitting behind the driver on the edge of the seat of this minivan, I tell him, "This isn't right!" He acts like he doesn't understand. I slap him several times on the shoulder. "Please! This isn't the right way!" There's a sinister feeling in this cab. Like he doesn't want me to get there right away.

"It's okay. Don't wurr-rry," he smiles at me in his rearview.

Why is he doing this? And going so slowly?

The physical need to touch Natalee overwhelms me. Both fists are flexing open, then shut, then stretched open again. I want to hug her. Hold her. Touch her hair. Take her home. I reach down between the seat and the console to push on the gas pedal with my hand. Carol, Sue, and Martee try to calm me. But I'm frantic. The police spokesman who just called has her picture. He must know this is Natalee. And Julia is a reporter. She certainly has photos of Natalee, because she has used them in her newspaper. She *must* know this is really her. It's the same anxiety experienced at the Buccaneer restaurant a few nights ago—only a hundredfold. My heart may come right through my chest as it travels from my throat to my feet and back again. Hurry. Just hurry.

We finally arrive to see multitudes of people standing outside of the dark police station. We are the *last ones here*. Again. The internal island communication system, their covert human network, is apparently fully operational tonight. Everyone present is either a native islander or with the media. They all knew to be here before we even got the call. *They all knew.*

Jug meets me, and together we walk up to the front door of the same police station where I gave my statement and confronted Vader a.k.a. Theodore a few days ago. We are the only two allowed inside. Everyone else waits outside. It's dim in the small waiting room. I am pacing. Again made to wait. Forever. A half hour passes, and no one is talking to us. I use this time to reassure, if not convince, myself that this must be the end of this wretched journey. So after this many days I can hold it together for at least a few more minutes. The people who told us to be here know what Natalee looks like. And maybe she is here and has told them her name herself! Still no one is in sight. I keep looking toward the office area behind the short swinging counter door to see someone—anyone—coming our way. We are alone. Waiting. In semidarkness. Waiting. Until finally I lose my momentum for urgency and sit down in one of the blue plastic chairs.

More time passes. Then from the left a door opens, and detective Jacobs brings a woman out. Jug and I don't move. She looks like she could be an American. She has very dark hair. We don't know if she's a tourist or if she lives here, but she looks nothing like Natalee. And she is coked or cracked out of her mind. A smirk across her face suggests that she knows she is part of some crazed drama. She's high on drugs, and her head bobs like one of those bobble-headed dogs on a dashboard.

I can't believe I even let myself experience another feeling of "This is it." Why do I do this?

The answer must be hope. What else could sustain a person to endure all this? Hope is the reason I believed Natalee was going to come through that door. Hope is why we react the way we do at all of these strange and excruciating and ultimately disappointing occurrences. It's that glimmer of a promise that the answer will be revealed.

Did the authorities make us wait so long because they realized it wasn't Natalee and were dreading the charade? Did they see it wasn't her, but had to put on the show anyway because of all the anxious onlookers outside?

Silent, Jug and I simply walk out of the police station and go our separate ways. The women return to the hotel for an hour or two of rest. Jug rejoins the crack-house and brothel search. All the positive energy created with the unity of hundreds of people over the last day or two expires in one long exhalation. And my very swollen, unrecognizable face, photographed leaving the Bubali station soon appears in the media.

————

ONE WEEK AGO THIS DAY Natalee was making plans with her friends to spend her last night in Aruba at Carlos 'n Charlie's. She left there with Joran van der Sloot and hasn't been seen since. Early this morning two dark-skinned native Aruban security guards from the Allegro Hotel are arrested in connection with Natalee's disappearance. Surely a result of yesterday's room-by-room search of that hotel. Their clothes are taken. Their cars are impounded. Potential evidence is removed from their homes. They are handcuffed and perp-walked to police cars and taken away. These security guards are labeled on the news as suspects in Natalee's disappearance. Apparently it's not difficult to get a search warrant for these two. But one certainly could not be obtained last week as we stood in the front yard of Joran van der Sloot's house as he told of his sexual encounter with Natalee. His father, Paulus, refused to let anyone inside their house, including the police.

Natalee never returned to the Holiday Inn. We saw the tapes with a room full of police officials. These two security guards also do not appear on the Holiday Inn security videos that we were shown. So why these arrests? Islanders are outraged. And so are we. It's blatant discrimination.

As we continue to move yet further away from the young men with whom Natalee was last seen, we are well aware that valuable evidence that could have been gathered that first morning is slowly and tragically being lost. Police didn't take the clothes from van der Sloot. They didn't search his house. They didn't arrest him after he lied to police right there in his front yard about taking Natalee back to the Holiday Inn. They haven't labeled him or the Kalpoe brothers as suspects. The car belonging to Deepak Kalpoe has not been impounded. And forensic tests have not been done. There might be evidence there.

Everywhere.

But we can't get the police to focus on the obvious. And finally we learn from the Wyndham Hotel manager that Joran and Deepak do not appear on their security videos at the time the two claimed to be at a poker tournament there—the same time we were standing in the van der Sloots' front yard in the wee hours of May 30.

"Something's wrong," I half whisper to Jug, following the arrests of the two security guards, and ask him to find an office supply store so we can have notebooks, paper, and pens to document these bizarre events. I've been taking scrap notes all along, but now begin to write down in a notebook every single thing that happens, word for word, from this day forward.

A few days ago we made a broadcast plea to Aruba to invite the FBI to help with Natalee's investigation. Now in addition to agent Shipley the FBI sends Kathleen here, a victim assistance specialist, to offer the family guidance and emotional support. We go over the notes we have been taking with her. She is sincere and very helpful. But our number-one question is, *How involved is the FBI in Natalee's investigation?*

"They are not doing a separate investigation," she tells us.

And we ask her if the Bureau is really being allowed to actively participate.

Kathleen says, "The police have been very kind and forthcoming, but they don't want to give out information."

We finally get to meet the vice-consul from the U.S. Consulate General office today. Five days after Natalee's disappearance. But she can't do much more than help us get names and addresses of government officials, so we can contact them ourselves and beg for help.

Everyone is journaling now, as much for therapy as for documentation. Sue writes that I'm "argumentative and hard to get along with today."

In the coming week the media scout for information on what my mood is before they ask me any questions. Anger and sadness rise sharply and fall steeply. Up and down as rapidly and profoundly as a heart monitor measuring each beat.

The arrest yesterday of the two security guards is so obviously a move in the wrong direction. My cursing is fluid and intense. I'm challenging God and His power to help me. Jug asks me to pray with him. "I'm not praying, Jug. You pray. Because it isn't working." He is so sad. Feeling helpless, totally helpless. As we pass Natalee's poster on the bulletin board by her room every night, I pause to give her a kiss. Tell her to be patient. Jug stays by my side, tolerating the news interviews, enduring the circus that has developed.

There's nothing any of us can do to help Natalee. We've run all over the place in all directions. In circles. Looking for her in restaurants, crack houses, whorehouses, on the beach, at the lighthouse. With Wendy and Peter Pan, O.J., Vader, and a bunch of other wacky characters. As the authorities watch.

Tips lead everywhere *except* toward those three young men. In spite of their lies and conflicting stories about the circumstances of the night in question, we can't get to them. We've been running up and down a football field for many days and nights now. We get a call—"She's here!"—and run from one end zone to the other. Then we get another call—"She's here!"—and run back to the opposite end of the field. "Here's a bloody mattress!" We run. "Here's a body!" We run. Back and forth. Back and forth.

Panic attacks come in waves over the next several days. They start with my mind racing backward. That's what I can't handle. I can't handle thinking back to how things were just a couple of weeks ago, when Natalee was at home. Safe. Happy. Getting ready to go to college. I have to only think forward, about the work at hand. And I can't process all the wonderful things people are doing for us here and back home. It's too overwhelming, because I don't know how I will ever thank everyone.

All these thoughts simply have to be kept behind a little door in my mind that I can only peek in momentarily and then close. If thoughts start to go back, it's like the rapid-fire flipping of a phone book. Control is lost, and dizziness sets in. Then sheer panic. And it's hard to breathe.

Kathleen, the FBI victim assistance specialist, tries to help me through these days with her comforting soft tone and encouraging words. She tells me maybe it's time to go home. But that's the last thing I intend to do. I can't leave Natalee here. Won't. I learn to recognize the signs of a panic attack and mentally fend it off.

Concerned family and friends send mild tranquilizers like Xanax and Valium. The collection of pills continues to grow as each new team arrives. But I don't tolerate painkillers well. And I'm so close to losing control that I'm afraid taking these pills will make me even worse. So I don't take them. I want to remain alert for Natalee, in case a call comes in. In case there's news. Just in case.

The only things that help are the beautiful messages of hope starting to stream in. People send their favorite scriptures, like Psalm 86:7:

> In the day of my trouble I call on you, for you will answer me.

And Romans 5:1–5:

> Therefore since we have been justified through faith, we have peace with God through our Lord Jesus Christ, through whom we have gained access by faith into this grace in which we now stand. And we rejoice in the hope of the glory of God. Not only so, but we also rejoice in our sufferings, because we know that suffering produces endurance, and endurance produces character, and character produces hope, and hope does not disappoint us ...

These powerful words quiet my mind and help me understand that an answer will come. And warm peace blankets me like it did that morning on the hillside at the cross as I think about Natalee's relationship with God. She is praying. Wherever she is.

Pocket angels, pocket crosses, prayer cards, notes, and hundreds more of the colorful prayer bracelets are hand delivered by Marcie, Cheryl, and Cindy—the new tag team.

Marcie, a devout Catholic, teaches me to pray the rosary. A Methodist praying the rosary! I find the repetition and the prayers very comforting. Every day I wear rosary beads, crosses, and stars around my neck. Prayer bracelets cover my arms. I suit up with religious symbols and fill my pockets with them as I head out to work for Natalee. These give me something to hold on to. Even though I trust God, I still can't see faith. So I rely on these treasures as the evidence of things unseen. As it says in Hebrews 11:1. And they give me great hope.

The most beautiful handmade prayer shawls arrive from some ladies in Talladega. Knitted and so soft, one is the most beautiful color of aqua blue I have ever seen. Another one is made from earth-tone colors of warm beige and cream. These shawls are long enough to wrap up in and provide immense physical comfort while the encouraging words offer spiritual reassurance. Wrapping up in a shawl, I sit on Natalee's bed to read the letters and uncover a small wrinkled note from one of my students, a child with autism. She etches out the words, "I love Natalee so much." That means the world to me. Being able to physically hold on to these symbols of hope, the tangible evidence of faith that sustains me, gives me peace. It's a feeling of calm in my heart even amid all the turmoil we're in. All these special heartfelt notes are kept safely tucked in the beautiful leather-bound Bible sent from Marcia. These words of hope lead me back to prayer. God *is* working. It's just hard to see the blessings for the despair.

Misery doesn't love company. I would never want anyone else to ever feel what I'm feeling. Misery loves comfort. And the words and actions of others are so comforting to us. News anchor Harris Faulkner is the first one to reach out with creature comforts. She brings me a big woven tote bag full of soothing lotions and soaps. And I'm so surprised! Not because someone did something thoughtful, but because I didn't know I was "allowed" to take comfort like this in the situation I'm in. It's like she is giving me permission to do something nice for myself. She unknowingly releases me from a self-imposed restriction. In a few days I seek comfort in these products, and they soothe me. And I am grateful for this profoundly positive step that lets me know it's okay to want to feel good.

The faithful Arubans are holding evening prayer services at the lighthouse. Volunteers meet in the Holiday Inn hotel lobby at ten o'clock every morning to go out on searches. Aruban government employees are given half a day off to scour the land to help. The international unity of hearts that so energized us a few days ago brings the mission back in focus.

Then finally, ten days after Natalee's disappearance, our prayers are answered. The police move in the right direction. They arrest Joran van der Sloot and Deepak and Satish Kalpoe on suspicion of kidnapping and murder. The suspects had ten days to cover their tracks. Ten days to corroborate their stories. And ten days to lawyer up.

The Bullet

Blood is pooling on the linoleum floor from the injection site in my arm. The young female Aruban technician is struggling with the vials that will hold my DNA samples. One will be sent to the Netherlands and one to the FBI crime lab in Quantico, Virginia. The FBI forensic specialist with me is irritated with the bumbling technician, and he asks her to remove the rubber band from my arm. A good deal of blood is on the floor now. But it has stopped coming from the site. She gets her sample and suggests to him that if he needs to get blood, there is some on the floor. Disgusted, the agent responds that they don't take blood samples off the floor. He injects me again to fill his vials. It's very hot and stuffy in this medical-center conference room. This blood loss coupled with the heat and a very heavy period cause me to feel faint. I make my way to the bathroom. And black out.

Aruba has not decided yet if it will invite the FBI to interrogate Joran van der Sloot and the Kalpoes now that they're in custody. As a sovereign nation, it decides who can participate in the investigation and who cannot. The prosecuting attorney, Karin Janssen, has to rely on police chief van der Straten for her information. He's in charge of the investigation and collects the materials to hand over to her.

I'm told even the Dutch investigators and interrogators from Holland have to be deputized to work on this island. Aruba calls its own shots. It's as if we're all on the outside. The FBI is willing to do anything Aruba *asks* them to do. That's how it has to be. Aruba has to ask. The FBI has outstanding state-of-the-art tools of the investigative trade ready to offer. But the request isn't made. The best the FBI can do is put things in place in the event it is allowed to participate in Natalee's investigation at some point.

After ten days Deepak's car is finally impounded. Also, Joran's private apartment at the van der Sloot home is finally searched. But not the whole house. Now the FBI has my DNA on file so it can be compared with evidence that might be collected.

Following yesterday's arrests of Joran van der Sloot and the Kalpoes, the media are in a frenzy as they become sucked into the bizarre-tip fiasco. Now I see them running here and running there. Following every crazy lead as we have done. At the dump it's rumored that a body has been found, and that Dave and I are arguing over whether or not it's Natalee. Reporters run for the dump. To get the story first.

"Beth, how are things today?" It's Diane Sawyer calling. She checks in on us frequently, and usually when I'm out putting up posters.

"We're still hopeful, Diane. Maybe someone will come forward with some information. Right now we're hanging reward posters." She and so many other popular newspeople call us daily. Hannah Storm even sent flowers. And it's incredibly reassuring.

The best thing the women and I can do is continue our mission to put up posters. Now that the suspects are in custody, maybe someone will feel more comfortable speaking up about what they know. We make our way throughout the island and finally all the way down to San Nicolas before returning to the hotel.

At the Holiday Inn the nightly meeting in the 007 room with FBI legal attaché Doug Shipley is about to get under way. Doug is an impeccably dressed, very professional man. Very FBI-ish. Anxious to hear what he has to say, we also want to tell him what we have learned about the professional relationship between Paulus van der Sloot and police chief van der Straten. Many people on the island have also told us that there is a personal relationship between the two as well, but we have no way of verifying this information. A private investigator hired by the family told me that Paulus van der Sloot was on an administrative judge's panel in 1996 or 1997. The investigator said while Paulus was on this panel the police chief worked for him and "had to answer to him."

We expect Doug will tell us what they've learned since the three arrests yesterday. Maybe they were able to get an idea of where these young men took Natalee. And we can go get her. But we didn't at all expect him to say what he did.

The 007 room is just a hotel room with no beds. There are some chairs, and Doug usually sits about three feet from me. He is usually forthright, businesslike, somewhat expressionless. But this time it's different. This time he slides his chair up next to me almost knee to knee. He gets eye to eye, as if we are the only two people in the room. This message is for me. Close up. Face-to-face.

"The way these guys are pointing the finger at each other, we're afraid there is a possibility that Natalee may not be alive."

And with that a bullet strikes me right in the gut. Takes my breath away. It's packed with birdshot, and the little pellets spread out all through my body, piercing my chest, my heart, my head, until I can't see straight. Everyone in the room witnesses this reaction. Sees the pain. Feels it. And there's nothing they can do. We believed we had at least a fifty-fifty chance of finding Natalee alive until these words are spoken. All the tips that she was seen here and there gave us hope. Until Doug carries out the dreaded job no one wants to do. He tells the parent who has to be told. Fires a bullet to the gut. And right here and now I vow to take Natalee's story to every high-school podium in the United States and do whatever I can to try to keep another family from experiencing our unbearable, unimaginable pain.

The tip line goes quiet almost as soon as Joran and the Kalpoes are in police custody. And the live sightings of Natalee all but cease. The volunteer search party that departs from the hotel lobby every morning is discontinued for now. People are instead asked to hand out yellow bows and ribbons, as they're doing back home. There's a general feeling that the police have their men now. And it doesn't take long for the media to report that *something bad has happened to Natalee.*

Every morning after the five o-clock news interviews and every night around midnight after our work is done, we go to the Alto Vista chapel to gather strength. When I step onto the chapel grounds it feels still. And calm. There is an undercurrent of evil present elsewhere, but not here. Being here takes all the bad things away for a little while. I actually feel this relief beneath my feet from the moment I arrive. Taking refuge here now in the face of the devastating news from the FBI, I lie on the ground and beg, "God, please take me instead!" Death doesn't scare me. Nothing could be worse than this. I would gladly take Natalee's place. I begin to wonder if her dead body has been lying some-where, hidden somewhere, on this island all along. And every-one knew.

"She'll be back ..." "Go wait at Carlos 'n Charlie's ..." "All missing girls at choller house ..."

Maybe they knew she was dead, but kept up the search game. No admission of a crime means no black mark. My brother Paul calls my mother to tell her. Then he tells his chil-dren, Natalee's little cousins. Our families begin to break the news to one another that there is a possibility that Natalee is dead. And we prepare to grieve.

I've learned in the past week and a half to give myself time to let information be absorbed. It's very challenging to decipher what is real here and what isn't. Lies blow across this island like the strong wind. In all directions. Stirring everything up. I need peacetime to figure out what to do.

After a couple of hours at the chapel, we return to the hotel to find that the tip line has become active again. Only now it's body sightings that are being reported. And all night long people bang on Natalee's hotel room door and call on the phone to tell us they know where her body is. And all night long FBI attaché Doug Shipley tells us that these reports aren't true. These terrorizing tips continue into the next day. And I retreat out of sight. All day. Away from the chaos.

Martee gets a Jeep for Sue, Carol, and me, and we go up onto the hillside between the lighthouse and the chapel. Just riding on off-road trails. Time to think. The terrain is barren and rocky, but the view over the rough sea is quite beautiful. And I find that looking at the water doesn't trouble me as much as it did the first week. Off to the side of the road are multitudes of little stacks of stones that progress into the distance along the cliff's shoreline. Statues are everywhere. These effigies, or human models, are left here by tourists as a symbol that they passed this way. The rows and rows of short stone towers create the appearance of a cemetery. The three other women mold a rock figure. But to me it's a creepy creation, cultlike. And I find the statues disturbing, eerie.

There's no talking as the Jeep crawls over the brutal terrain. Only the sound of the engine occasionally revving up to climb over rocks. And the tires crackling over gravel.

Sue's voice breaks the hypnotic sounds. "Beth, do *you* think Natalee is dead?"

It takes me a minute or so to answer. Then, reluctantly, I respond, "Yeah ..." with a deep and heavy sigh. "I think she's gone."

Sue bursts into tears.

I'm weak with sadness. Empty after hearing Doug Shipley's words. We all are. It's all I can do to sit up in the jeep. All I can do to breathe in. To survive this day I have to reach for something, anything. And hope evolves from the desperate need to find Natalee to simply the desperate need for an answer. Whatever it is. Just hope for an answer.

The theory that Natalee has been murdered swells to a great crescendo throughout the day. Geraldo reports live on the air with Jug and me standing next to him that Aruban prime minister Oduber says there is blood in Deepak's car. A luminal test revealed "something" on the interior. Parts of the seat and interior roof are cut out and sent to the Dutch Forensic Institute for further tests. This is the first we hear of this. The prime minister then says he expects the case to be solved tomorrow. Soon the headlines in the Aruban newspaper *Diario* read, "Deepak Raped and Buried Natalee ..." All accounts point to the three suspects. The newspaper publisher, Jossy Mansur, tells FOX's Greta Van Susteren that Joran broke down and cried during his interrogations and confessed to police that they buried Natalee. Reports of a murder confession are rampant.

But not long after, all this information is called back. Retracted! A government spokesman who stated that Natalee was confirmed dead claims he was caught up in a "misinformation campaign." It's a pathetic spectacle of ineptness and incompetence. Confession. No confession. She's dead. She's not dead.

We're barely holding ourselves together. The cruelty is as hard to comprehend as the sheer confusion of it all. Who is pulling the strings? Who controls Aruba? *Who is the Wizard?* The mafia and drug cartels? We sense that a dark influence controls the actions of some. And some officials elected by the good people of Aruba are prevented from doing their jobs, maybe threatened. And all the confusion of the day leads us back to the hope that there is still a fifty-fifty chance that Natalee is alive. Somewhere. On this island.

My poor mother hears on the news that there is a murder charge and calls me, very, very upset. "No, Mom. It's different here. What we call charges and what they call charges aren't the same. The three are under 'suspicion' ... Yes, there was a rumor about a confession ... The authorities changed their minds on that ... The three are still suspects though. It's just different here."

I know it's hard for her to understand. It's hard for everyone. Dutch law is very complicated. As I'm sure American law would be for an Aruban caught in a crisis in the United States. But as Americans, we have certain expectations. Like truth, for instance. And accountability. In our justice system we have checks and balances to diffuse the potential for corruption. And we try to get to the bottom of crimes with tools like the plea-bargain agreement and the polygraph test among a multitude of other advanced crime-fighting technologies. But there's no plea bargain in Aruba. And no polygraphing.

When we find ourselves in a crisis in a country that promotes itself as a tourist haven for Americans, we naively expect to get the same kind of help and justice that we would get at home. But that's idealistic. When Americans leave the United States, we should be prepared to leave behind all those expectations of being treated with the same fairness and dignity we are accustomed to and take for granted. It's one thing to be lost in the United States. It's another whole disaster to be lost in another country. You must adhere to the government, police, laws, and customs of the country you're visiting. And they're just not the same as ours.

On top of all these barriers, we find out that the "invitation" Aruba made to the FBI to participate in Natalee's case was basically all lip service. We learn that the FBI is kept at arm's length and is not allowed a hands-on role in the investigation. Its agents are only here as invited guests. They can be observers, and that's all. So far, law enforcement from Natalee's homeland can't do anything concrete to help her. Not the FBI. Not the DEA. Not Homeland Security. Not senators or representatives.

That's why we need a lawyer. An Aruban lawyer. Someone who can navigate us through the Dutch legal system. Intercede to help us get information, communicate with us. Let us know where the investigation stands, help straighten out the conflicting reports. Even if the police were talking to us, it probably wouldn't matter because they don't seem to know what's going on. When we ask for things, such as the phone number for the investigative team, for instance, the response is that they don't have it. It takes us weeks to realize that it seems the police don't communicate with the prime minister, and it also appears the prime minister doesn't communicate with the attorney general. And after many attempts to reach the minister of justice, the man who we are told is ultimately responsible for cases like Natalee's on this island, he has yet to respond to our pleas for help. It appears no one wants to accept responsibility for Natalee's investigation. It's like the scene in the movie in which Dorothy comes upon the Scarecrow to ask for directions. He points in one direction, then another, and finally his arms cross and he points in opposite directions at the same time. That's how it feels here.

We're fortunate that one of the men from home here to help us is an attorney, so he personally interviews several Aruban lawyers and decides Vinda de Sousa will be as good as any. Her retainer is $5,000 up front. Within a week or two she makes it possible for us to hear a translation of the statement Joran van der Sloot gave when he was taken into custody on June 9. Jug, Dave, and I go with Vinda to attorney general Theresa Croes's office. There, prosecuting attorney Karin Janssen comes in and lays a stack of statements on the conference table in front of us. Vinda's assistant rifles through them and begins to read one given by Joran van der Sloot, translating from Dutch to English. Prosecutor Janssen leaves the room. We are not told what the interrogator asks, but these are Joran's words, his responses, of June 9, 2005. We are not allowed to have copies, so I write it all down:

On May 29 I was at the Texas Hold 'Em table at the Excelsior at 4:00 [p.m.] with my father. I lost, and we left [the table] between 7:00 and 8:00 p.m. I went to the blackjack table. This is where I met Natalee and her friends. Friends kept insisting for me to come to Carlos 'n Charlie's. After this the girls left for the bar. I called my father at 11:00 p.m. to come pick me up at McDonald's.

Deepak and Satish came to pick me up at 12:30 a.m. on May 30 to take me to Carlos 'n Charlie's. I did sneak out. I have a VIP pass to go there that allows me to invite all guests in. I go there two times weekly. When I enter Natalee is dancing on the stage. Her friends say, "Natalee has an eye on you," and they want me to dance. Natalee was not drinking. I order a yard whiskey coke. Natalee wanted me to do a Jell-O shot on her stomach. So she lay down on the bar so I could do it. I felt she had been drinking. Natalee wanted to continue drinking. I paid $20 for two shots of [rum] 151. She drank a shot. Satish was standing next to her. She followed the shot with a chaser of whiskey coke.

After, Natalee, Satish, and I walk outside. Everyone was leaving. Natalee said she wanted me to take her to my house. Around 1:15 we walked from Carlos 'n Charlie's with Satish. Deepak was waiting in the car. Deepak was driving. Satish was a passenger. Natalee asked them if they were rich. She was impressed by their car. She also yelled "Aruba" out of the window to her friends. A friend told her two times to get out of the car.

We took her to the lighthouse because she wanted to see sharks. She put her hand on my leg, and we started kissing. She kept falling asleep and waking up. I began kissing her again. She put her hand on my penis. I caressed her breasts. She is shaven. First, I placed my middle finger in her and then the rest. I still continue kissing her. She asked if they were my slaves.

Her underwear was dark blue with embroidered flowers. I was fingering Natalee, and Deepak and Satish and me were in the car. Natalee fell asleep and woke up. Then wanted to go home. No more kissing. We drove up to the lighthouse and around the sand dunes, then back to the Holiday Inn. Deepak parked on the left side. Natalee got out of the car, and the guards came up.

This is the first of several statements Joran makes. And no two are ever the same. They are so nasty and so painful to hear. What troubles me in this statement, besides the obvious fact that this suspect has had sexual contact with my semiconscious daughter, is the report of Natalee's constant falling asleep and waking up. Natalee had consumed alcohol according to friends. And if she consumed the 151 rum, it would certainly have been enough to cause her to become even more intoxicated. But to fall asleep and wake up, fall asleep and wake up like that tells me there's more to it. It's my belief that whatever she consumed was tampered with. Something was put in her drink. The crazy things she reportedly was saying convince me even more that she was drugged.

The next day Joran was questioned at least twice. There were tips that the Kalpoe brothers were seen washing their car, scrubbing it inside and out, in the wee hours of the morning of May 30, the same morning Natalee disappeared with them. So why did they decide to wash it at three-thirty or four o'clock in the morning of the day Natalee disappeared? Were they washing out blood? Vomit? What are the results of the samples taken from the interior of Deepak's car? The prosecutor says they were sent to the Dutch Forensic Institute. And she later reports to us that the findings from the luminal test showed "cleaning fluid, not blood." Cleaning fluid.

Joran was asked how Deepak keeps his car and about his own social habits. These are his words from two-thirty in the afternoon on June 10, 2005:

> The car was clean. I mostly sit in the front. I've been drinking since I was fifteen, mostly a social drinker. I drink a case just to get tipsy. It would take twenty to thirty glasses before I get drunk. Mom is lying like hell. When I get drunk, I get tired and go to sleep. If Deepak drinks, he becomes very aggressive and irritated. He gets very mad quickly. Koen's father has a boat.
>
> Deepak and Satish typically don't date girls. I'm under a psychologist. I'm doing this because the girl was missing, and I had been seeing a psychologist. My father warned me not to talk on cell phones.

In this brief he states out of the clear blue that "Koen's father has a boat." Koen is a friend of Joran's. Because we aren't privy to the interrogator's questions, we don't know why he is volunteering that his friend's father has a boat. We also don't know why he is offering information about instructions from his father.

The most startling and stunning revelations come out in Joran's statement taken at seven-thirty in the evening on the same day, June 10, 2005:

> Now I am going to tell you. We drove to my house. I was kissing Natalee. Deepak is driving. I wanted to go back to the hotel. At 1:40 in the morning on May 30 Deepak dropped me off at home. I went to my room while Deepak and Satish took her home. I called Deepak at 3:00 a.m. to tell him I'm home. Then I called Deepak at 3:30 and ask him, "How's it going? Did you drop the girl off at the Holiday Inn?"

Here, Joran says Deepak took him home at one-forty in the morning, yet he feels the need to call Deepak an hour and a half later to say that he's home! Also in this statement Joran says it's the Kalpoes who are left alone with Natalee. And his elaborate description of how he and Deepak left her at the Holiday Inn, the one he dramatically reenacted for all of us that first morning, is never mentioned. Joran continues this statement:

> My father told us that our e-mails would be read and our cell phones would be bugged. He told us to get our stories straight and then send e-mails. We should use the hard drive to nail an alibi. First, all three of us have to agree on the story and stick to it. If we keep calm and all

our stories match, they will let us go in ten days. My father said to me, "I hope she is alive. But not a big chance for that."

"Not a big chance for that." It's even worse than we thought as we hear Joran declaring that his father has instructed all three suspects on covering their tracks. AP reports that Paulus van der Sloot gave his son and the Kalpoes legal advice the day after Natalee disappeared. In this same report it's stated that Aruba's attorney general says Paulus told the three young men "when there is no body you don't have a case."

The prime suspect, Joran, is questioned again on June 11, 2005. When asked to cooperate with the police on this date he simply says, "No statement. This is the whole truth. No more."

Then two days later, on June 13, 2005, Joran declares that his previous statements are not true and offers this account:

My third statement is not true. Now the truth. We drove to my house at 1:40 a.m. on May 30. I want her to come in. I have sex with her. Next, we go to the beach and walk to the fishermen's huts. We kiss and she masturbates me. After I'm done, I told her to go back to the Holiday Inn, but she wanted to stay there on the beach. I called Deepak to pick me up at the fishermen's huts at 3:30 a.m. She still wanted to stay there. Deepak said, "Don't f–k with that bitch. Let's go." He asked me, "What did you do with Natalee?"

Seeing it in black and white on the paper, the conflicting stories, the lies, I realize that the crazy things that happened in the past two weeks are probably all true. Something bad *did* happen to Natalee. And all the information about blood in Deepak's car and a supposed murder confession that was labeled "misinformation" is also probably true. And we have no idea what has become of all this information.

Joran's statements are very, very difficult to listen to—the words of the one held on suspicion of kidnapping and murdering my daughter. Her alleged assailant. Giving very different versions every time he is interrogated. I feel like throwing up. But if I succumb to emotion, I won't be able to get all the words down. So I detach. Keep writing. Vinda's assistant next pulls Deepak's statement out of the pile. It was also taken June 13, 2005. These are Deepak's words:

> Joran's father asked me if I had a lawyer. He is getting worried because the case is getting serious. He told me not to worry, that he will look for a lawyer for me. He is hiring one for me.
>
> My brother Satish and I went to Joran's house to talk to his father there. He told us what to do.

We are asked to withhold all this information because it could compromise the investigation; asked not to discuss it with the media or anyone. And we comply. We're trying to play by their rules. For me, this is the one true set of statements shared with us in the attorney general's office. We have heard the conflicting words, the inconsistent accounts. And after seeing the torn statement in the Bubali police station that had Joran van der Sloot's name on it, there's no telling what will become of these statements. Ironically, the truth about what happened to Natalee is somewhere in these lies. She most likely was never taken to any of the places the suspects name in their statements. Not the lighthouse. Not the fishermen's huts. Not the beach. Not the Holiday Inn. But I do think she was taken to the van der Sloots' home. And I believe that whatever happened to her, happened there.

A fourth suspect, a party-boat deejay, is detained after he steps up to support the story that Joran and the Kalpoes left Natalee at the Holiday Inn. He is also lying. Apparently he didn't get the memo that the Holiday Inn drop-off story was already replaced by the we-left-her-at-the-beach story.

When Jug, Dave, and I walk out of the attorney general's office, we are 1,000 percent certain. We've got 'em. They did it. It's all there. And we all agree that there is no way any of these three will ever be released.

THIS DAY TURNS OUT TO BE even harder than getting the bullet in the gut. And my spirit yearns for some reassurance that it will survive this ordeal. A special service is being held for Natalee tonight. The passionate and faithful native Arubans hold prayer services quite often, and we attend different churches almost every day as time allows. We're so grateful for the support they have shown us in our time of need.

Tonight we visit a multidenominational congregation. Eleven ministers, men and women, mostly Pentecostal, are present at this service. They have a special seat for me in the first row. The service begins with beautiful music, and the soloist is incredible, her voice soothing. Hearing "How Great Thou Art" in Papiamento, I think about Mom and our roots in the Methodist Church. This is one of her favorite hymns. Mine too. The words sound different in this language, but still mean the same. There is comfort in this familiarity. And the tone is set for the minister to begin his sermon. The words he says could have just as easily come from our hometown church leaders. He speaks to Natalee and to me. It's as if he has known her all of her life.

Following the sermon, the service continues with some heavy-duty praying. I mean we are praying. Silently or out loud. Arms raised, outstretched, or hands quietly folded. And I hear something that isn't Papiamento. And it isn't Dutch. I can't put my finger on it. Then I realize some of the church members are speaking in tongues. I've heard of this, but never actually experienced it. It's mysterious and captivating. A little scary at first. As all this is taking place the eleven ministers extend their hands for me to come to the front and stand in the middle of a circle they have formed. With my eyes closed for almost the entire ceremony, the voices in tongues create a soft chorus in the background behind me.

I let go of denominational preconceptions and just experience the love and safety of the spiritual cocoon in which they've enveloped me. They lay their hands on me. On my shoulders, my back, my head. And I sense that I am lifted up. Literally. My emotions alternate between crying and peace. Then total calm comes, and I am overwhelmed with the sense of oneness. The realization that we're all the same no matter where we go.

At this moment there are no Americans. No Arubans. No Dutch. We're all one in His world. Governments and political systems might not make us feel valuable, but we make each other feel valuable, worthy of prayer and comfort. I understand that I am one with other suffering parents and that their pain is mine. And mine theirs. The soldier's father. The student's mother. We're all the same. Parents. All the same. None of us is exempt from the profound agony that comes from the loss of a child. And thankfully, none of us is excluded from His love. Mom is still right. God is good. Grief is suddenly accompanied by relief. At peace in this field of love, I pray for other parents who are suffering like me.

———————

FRENCH PHILOSOPHER PIERRE TEILHARD DE CHARDIN is quoted as saying, "We are not human beings having a spiritual experience; we are spiritual beings having a human experience." This intuitive and deep reflection of who we are and why we're here on this earth stays with me throughout the course of this tragedy. And it helps me make some sense out of the madness in this world. 9/11. War. The death and loss of children. A lot of people have a lot of pain to endure. And one person's life is no more important than another's. The philosopher's statement reminds me that we're just passing through on this human journey, that *this* is the hard part, and that there is a promise of more to come.

I think about the sermon delivered by Rabbi Jonathan Miller at Temple Emanu-El in Birmingham regarding Natalee's disappearance. He said, "Hope is the belief that things can be made right again." I agree. It may not be in this lifetime, but one day things will be made right. And my pain and the pain suffered by all people will end. I'd have no hope at all if I believed that this human existence was all there was.

Catch and Release

Everyone is leaving tomorrow as we move through the third week of Natalee's disappearance. All family members and friends. Even Carla, the New York public relations person who has been such tremendous help with the media. She is being "reassigned." The Aruba tourism officials reportedly complain that she has become too close to the family. Indeed. She and my brother Paul have become quite close. My friend Carol is coming back for the third time. Half the number of times she will eventually make this trip.

The mission of meeting people and handing out the Ecclesiastes prayer cards and the beautiful colorful bracelets gives me a reason to get up and keep going. FOX anchor Greta Van Susteren wants to come along, as many of the network reps have done over the past few weeks. We're going to the other end of the island today, near the van der Sloot neighborhood, to ask for information. And help.

As I reach to put a prayer card into the van der Sloot mailbox, I see someone on the side of the house and call out, "Anybody home? Hello! You've got company! Knock, knock! Anybody home?"

A man is behind the shrubs against the house.

"I see you there in the bushes."

He freezes.

"I'm Natalee's mom. I just want to give you a prayer card."

Paulus van der Sloot has to be coaxed out of the bushes like a dog in trouble. He appears from behind the shrubs and comes to the gate. I hand him one of Natalee's prayer cards over the fence.

Surprisingly, he says, "Come in, please. Stop the cameras, okay? Stop the cameras."

Greta and I lock eyes for a moment, and with no hint of hesitation on her part we go inside. Through the front door we make our way across the tile floor, passing through a nicely decorated living room, under an archway, to an enclosed back-porch area. We step down to a table and chairs. Paulus's wife, Joran's mother, Anita, is here. There's no glass in the multiple window openings in this room, just wooden slats. And the air moves comfortably through the area. The wind blows hard all the time in Aruba, and it's breezy in here, well ventilated. Paulus sits closest to the air flow. I sit across from him, in close proximity. Anita is on my left. Greta is next to Paulus, her body turned toward him.

Anita tells us all about Joran and what a good boy he is. How smart he is. I let her go on and on, as this gives me time to listen, look, assess. And as she continues, she begins to share with us what a difficult time they have had with him recently. How he exhibits oppositional defiance and is disrespectful to his mother. How they are beginning to lose control of him as he sneaks out at night and comes and goes as he pleases. After about thirty minutes she concludes by telling us Joran is seeing a psychologist for his defiant behavior.

Now it's my turn. I have no intention of matching her goodboy remarks with good-girl comments. And cut to the chase. Graphically repeating the very words said by their son a couple of weeks ago in his statements made on June 9, 10, and 13. The vile account that was read to me in the attorney general's office. The sexually explicit words used by Joran to describe what he did to Natalee. Calmer than I have ever been in my whole life and without blinking, I tell them which fingers he said he used. Where he said he put them. How their son described my daughter's pubic area, her underwear. How Joran said she was falling asleep and waking up, falling asleep and waking up. I tell them of his conflicting stories of what happened, the different places he said it happened. Little beads of sweat form across Paulus's brow and forehead.

My arms rest on top of the investigation notebook I carry with me all the time. Natalee's reward poster with her picture on it is inside the front clear cover, in plain view. Paulus's arms are on the table. Our knuckles are only inches apart. His arms are shaking. His fists are clenched.

"You're responsible for Aruba being trapped in hell," I tell him, still calm. "You can change that. But Aruba will stay in a perpetual state of hell until you come forward."

I gently push the notebook toward him so he can see Natalee. Anita remains silent. The breeze is blowing even cooler through the room now, yet the sweat on Paulus is increasing.

"How did Joran get home that night, Paulus?"

He responds that he doesn't know.

"Did he go to school the next day?"

He responds again that he doesn't know.

Greta and I have many questions. "You mean this is the most critical time in your son's life—he is being held on suspicion of kidnap and murder—and you don't know how he got home or if he went to school?"

Paulus stammers when he answers. He hesitates. He sounds unnatural and blinks rapidly. His head is down. The beads of sweat turn to bubbles that grow together and gather under his chin, then drop—splash—onto the table below.

Pulling a couple of prayer bracelets out of my pocket, I offer them to the van der Sloots. First I tie one on Anita's arm, then ask Paulus if he would like one. He lifts his clench-fisted arm, shaking as if he has Parkinson's disease, and tries very hard to hold it up. What a pathetic form of a man he is, I think—a very different person from the one who stood so brazenly in his front yard in the wee hours that first morning, facing down Aruban police and our men from home. I take my time tying the bracelet, very, very slowly, and explain the meaning of the three cords of yarn.

"Paulus, this bracelet stands for a Bible verse. It's Ecclesiastes 4:12. 'Though one may be overpowered, two can defend themselves. A cord of three strands is not quickly broken.'" I finish the tying and gently pat the knot. "There you go."

And right then the bracelet looks different to me. I see the three cords as the suspects, and the knot at the end holding them together as Paulus. It's not just clear—it's crystal clear. There are potentially four people who know what happened to Natalee. We need the knot to come loose and the three to unravel.

Anita gets a kitchen towel and first blots Paulus's head. Then she lays it on the pools of sweat that have formed on the table in front of him and, in one big swipe, folds the towel over and cleans it away.

A few days later Paulus is arrested and questioned by Aruban police after they say he changed his story about what time he picked up Joran on the night Natalee disappeared. First Paulus states that he picked *"them"* up at McDonald's at four in the morning on May 30. We do not know who he means by "them." Later he changes his story completely, saying he picked Joran up at eleven at night on May 29 at McDonald's. By making this change, his story now coincides with the one Joran gave police on June 9. But according to Aruban police officials it also makes Paulus another lying witness.

In Joran's statements of June 9 and 10 he never mentions any time that his father was involved in a pickup at McDonald's other than May 29 at eleven at night. Period. However, when I asked Paulus face-to-face how Joran got home that night, he said he didn't know.

No one could have predicted that this encounter would take place. And if Greta Van Susteren had not been there, I would not have gone inside.

———————

AFTER MORE THAN THREE WEEKS since Natalee's disappearance, the reward for her safe return is still increasing. All we can do is continue to search for her, for an answer, and try to keep the case alive. My brother Paul contacted a search team in Texas that has sonar equipment, dogs, drones, and experience. Tim Miller, who heads up Texas Equu-Search, and his team are here now, ready to go to work.

There are many, many locations on the island that we are not allowed to search. The luxurious homes up on the hilltops surrounded by very high walls are a concern for us, especially the ones with barbed wire around the top. We're told some of those are the mansions of the big drug lords. Others are brothels for the elite. And we can't go up there. We do get close enough to see where helicopters land. And, of course, it's very troubling. The more shady information like this that comes out, the more aggravated people become. The more aggravated they become, the more they want to try to help us.

Today help and hope are coming hand in hand from a famous fellow Mississippian.

"Hey, Beth. This is Brett Favre." Tim Miller told me that Brett asked how to reach us a few days ago. Brett has already offered support to the Texas Equu-Search team and is calling now with an extraordinary idea. He tells me he has learned something interesting from former president Bill Clinton, who, of course, hails from my home state of Arkansas. Mr. Clinton apparently has communicated with agents on the island who say there is a Green Bay Packers poster in Joran's room. Perhaps Joran looks up to Brett. The famous football star wants to come to the island to meet Joran in person to see if he can have an impact on the young suspect, maybe get him to tell the truth once and for all. Since one can apparently buy anything on this island except the answer to where Natalee is, an amount of money makes it possible for a face-to-face meeting between Joran, Brett, and me. Brett says he will be here on Saturday.

The meeting will take place on Monday at one o'clock in the interrogator's office. "A couple of people will travel with me," Brett says—he is going to ask Yao Ming and Peyton Manning to join him. I don't ask how or why or anything. I'm in. The only thing he asks is that we do not mention this to the media. Of course, when Yao Ming shows up at the Aruba airport, they'll all know. Brett says we'll deal with that when it happens. We have quite a long conversation, and he is very warm and sympathetic. He felt compelled to do *something* for his fellow Mississippians who are in crisis (Natalee's father, Dave, and his family who live there now, and Natalee, who was raised in Clinton).

A day or so later Brett reluctantly calls back to say that due to management concerns he is going to have to renege. He is apologetic. But it doesn't matter. He did the ultimate by reaching out to us. My son, Matt, and Jug's son, George, got to experience a few moments of great anticipation that a football hero was going to intercede on Natalee's behalf. Brett's offer was worth this alone. The fact that he even went so far as to attempt to help means so much.

Every down seems to be followed by an up. Hopelessness is again defeated by hope. And we trudge forward.

AN AP REPORT DATED July 1, 2005, reads: "Three young men detained in the disappearance of an Alabama teenager have been charged with murder since their arrest three weeks ago." Prosecutor Karin Janssen is quoted saying, "At the time we didn't want to upset the Holloway family by talking about murder while they searched ..."

The three suspects are being taken by police to the beach, so they can show them where they left Natalee, just to see if their stories match up. And in a few days a judge will make the decision whether the three will remain in custody or go free.

Knowing what we know, after hearing the suspects' statements in the attorney general's office, we can't help but feel optimistic. Continuing to establish ties with the island community helps the days pass. Today Betsy and Anola, the new helpers, are going into fourth- and fifth-grade Aruban classrooms with me to make prayer bracelets with the children. They cut yards and yards of yarn and teach the Ecclesiastes verse. This is an especially touching time for me. I find myself thinking of my students back home. These children are beautiful, precious. They are so curious about all the activity in their classroom today, which includes a team from *People* magazine, but they all seem to know about Natalee.

The native islanders are still behind us, which is evident in the human prayer chain facilitated by Father Tony. Tourists, islanders, and hotel employees—who are allowed to leave work for a few minutes to join the prayer—hold hands together in a chain that we are told stretches from the Holiday Inn to the Wyndham Hotel.

I can't see to the end of the line, but it's a remarkable show of faith and support. And we need it. Father Tony prays, "Lord, show us the way to Natalee, no matter how difficult it may be. Help us accept the truth about what happened to her no matter how bitter it may be. Please give us back Natalee alive. Amen."

IN THE STATES IT'S INDEPENDENCE DAY. At the Aruba courthouse we are not allowed to go inside the courtroom during the hearing. The media are present en masse. Competition among the networks is at an all-time high. Everyone wants to get the story first. Producers who at first shared satellite time and interview space are now very territorial. It's tense. And so very hot.

Time passes with no information. We move to our attorney's office to wait it out. Still no word. Anola cuts more yarn for the schoolchildren. "Every minute is like a day," Betsy observes. We move to a restaurant to pass even more time. Finally, a call. It's FBI attaché Doug Shipley. He says matter-of-factly, "The Kalpoes have been released." It happened an hour ago. Everyone claims they never saw this coming. Just a few days ago we heard the conflicting statements from Joran. We heard Deepak and him implicate Paulus in a conspiracy to hide a crime. Even police chief van der Straten says, "The suspects continue to change their stories every time they're interrogated. The three boys are guilty of involvement." Regardless, today is apparently independence day for two of the three suspects. And tomorrow Chief van der Straten will retire. He will be replaced by three police officials, one named Chief Deputy Gerold Dompig.

There's only one word to describe our reaction to the release of the Kalpoes, a word coined by my friend Marcie. It's a combination of astonishment and stunned—we are in astunment.

As Joran van der Sloot is taken from the courthouse, all smiles on his way back to jail, it feels as though everything is falling down around us. We can't get a break. In a meeting with prosecutor Janssen the day after the release, Jug's brother, Jar, asks her if she has a working theory.

"Yes," she says. "It was sex gone wrong."

He asks her who she believes is involved.

The prosecutor says, "Definitely Joran, and at least one of the Kalpoe brothers."

"So they were involved in a crime . . ." Jar continues.

"Yes," she answers.

"And they are free to move around the country now?"

"Yes," the prosecutor replies. "They are free to go wherever they want to go."

And in an instant all the up-and-down on the heart monitor stops. All the back-and-forth on the football field stops. I stop. And lie down on the fifty-yard line. Flat-lined. In a state of astunment.

The last thing we need is for two of the three individuals who might know what happened to Natalee to vaporize. We compose a statement and call a press conference. The media room is packed. I'm jammed behind a small lectern covered with microphones. It's hot. And I'm emotional when I ask other nations not to allow the Kalpoe brothers a safe haven. "Two suspects were released yesterday who were involved in a violent crime against my daughter. I am asking mothers and fathers in all nations to hear my plea. Do not allow the Kalpoe brothers to enter your country until this case is solved. Do not allow these criminals to walk among your citizens. Help me by not allowing these two to get away with this crime, in the name of my beautiful daughter whom I have not seen in thirty-six days and for whom I will continue to search until I find her."

No one is breathing. Or moving. Reporters and camerapeople are crying. The media have been here more than a month, and they've seen firsthand what we've experienced. They are moved by this plea. But some of the Arubans are not. Calling their local sons "criminals" offends them. Having just heard the prosecuting attorney tell us at least one of the Kalpoes could be involved in whatever happened to my daughter, I felt the term seemed appropriate. But it led to an abrupt change in the tide of support.

It was never my intention to offend the Arubans. I thought we were all on the same page. We were receiving such positive feedback from locals here that I was shocked when they reacted negatively to my using the word "criminals." But I unwittingly crossed that line between what family can say about family and what strangers can say about family. The Arubans would have done anything for us before this speech was delivered, and I'm so sad that this turn in support has taken place.

Not long after the "criminals speech," some Arubans back off their prayer vigils for Natalee. A few protest in the streets against the barrage of negative media. We've worn out our welcome at the Holiday Inn. And they let us know they've had it. The Aruba Tourism Authority (ATA), the Aruba Hotel and Tourism Association

(AHATA), the Aruba Trade and Industry Association, and a smat-
tering of island officials establish the Strategic Communications
Task Force to combat the negative media. And to combat us.

There's no question that Natalee made a tragic mistake when
she allowed herself to get in a condition and a situation in which
she could not choose her free will. But should it have cost her
her life? She allowed her judgment to become impaired by alcohol, and that left her unable to make her own choices. The decision to get in that car was made for her. When she was least able
to defend herself she was taken. Natalee let her guard down for
one moment. And in that moment she vanished.

If I leave Aruba, this case will vanish like Natalee did. I am
her voice for justice, for human rights, and I will stay to ride this
out. Joran's next court date is September 1. At that time he
should get thirty more days and that will take us to October 1.
Staying on this will consume the rest of the summer and early
fall, and Jug needs to go back to work. Preparing to settle in for a
longer period, I have to make the difficult decision to move out
of Natalee's hotel room. It's a major first step. A very hard one.

The Holiday Inn has very generously provided our family a
block of rooms free of charge for the six weeks we have been
here. We are very, very grateful for their hospitable gesture
beyond the call of duty. But it's time to move. The Wyndham
Hotel gives us a reduced room rate on a very nice suite. Having a
kitchenette will be very helpful, economically speaking as
well as for convenience, as we hunker down for the duration of
Natalee's case.

Many trips back and forth to the car are required to pack up the thousands of letters and special treasures from people and transport them to the Wyndham—flower arrangements, rosaries, crosses, Stars of David, medals, saints, Mass cards, prayer cards, prayer bracelets, heartfelt notes, letters, and special mementos. I wear the Star of David right next to the cross right next to the rosary every day. And I read every single note and letter as it arrives. These provide great comfort and remind me of the prayers that are being said for Natalee and her family from people of all faiths, from all over the world. Some letters are addressed simply to "Beth Holloway," but the U.S. Post Office amazingly gets them to Aruba. Somehow they find me.

———————

IN THE NEW ROOM NATALEE'S PICTURE takes its place on the bedside table, enshrined with treasures from caring people. With the light on. And I look forward to the nightly ritual of wrapping up in a prayer shawl to read the letters. My friend Sunny arrives to trade places with Anola and Betsy and joins me in the ceremony. Mickey Rourke sends a heartfelt message. Kathie Lee Gifford sends a beautiful, spiritual note with her CD. And she, like everyone else, encourages me to have hope and keep the faith. All the heartfelt, encouraging words give reassurance that we can persevere and stand strong until justice is served.

A man in California writes that he has never prayed before now, but he is praying for Natalee. He includes his number, and I have to call him. We establish a wonderful friendship. One night he calls to tell me how sick his mother is and that he prayed for her. He wants to know if it's okay that he feels relieved. He is unsure whether he is supposed to feel this way, and maybe even feels a little guilty for the relief prayer brings him.

"Yes. That's how it works," I explain. "You gave up the burden of worrying about your mother to God. It's okay to feel comforted."

We fold up our prayer shawls, carefully put the notes back in their envelopes, and turn in.

"Good night," Sunny says, reaching over to turn off her light.

"'Night," I reply. And in a minute or so I reach over and turn off mine. "Oooh, that's dark," I whisper.

And so ends the six-week vigil in Natalee's room. Sleeping in her bed, on her side, in one of her shirts. The lamp is off, but I know the light of hope still shines. And it's okay. It's okay.

Reality Reality TV

CNN's Nancy Grace coughs and chokes on the air to dramatize her reaction to the statement from an Aruban official that the suspects have given twenty-two versions of what happened to Natalee. Then she holds up a soup ladle and offers to help the island drain the pond faster. Authorities are working on emptying a pond following a tip from a gardener who says he saw the three suspects sitting in Deepak's car near this pond in the wee morning hours of May 30. Other bizarre discoveries such as blond hairs on duct tape, bones, and a barrel that is lugged onto shore by tourists also keep the media intrigued. All this goes on as forensic divers from Florida State University work the waters and Texas Equu-Search, though denied access to many areas on the island, works the land. Everyone wants the answer.

Friends at home send clothes because the few items I have are falling off. I've lost fifteen pounds in the past two months here. The majority of that came off in the first two weeks. The weight loss and the emotional stress are causing irregular uterine bleeding. It's constant between the cycles. Regardless of these detrimental physical reactions to all the stress, the equatorially intense Aruba heat feels good piercing my skin as I run along the sidewalk. And I can feel it through my tennis shoes under my feet. I want to feel it. The high noon heat, the sweat, the breathing. Exercising for the first time since being here feels good. Moving out of Natalee's room was a good thing after all. But I had to wait until I could do it on my own terms. Hurting people can't be pushed. Moving through a crisis is a process that runs on its own clock. And it's different for each one of us.

The Mountain Brook community is united to help us see this through. Natalee's friends raise $20,000 at a band fund-raiser held at Otey's, a local grill, another $1,000 at a snow-cone stand, and a couple thousand more at a cookout at Mountain Brook Community Church. Local radio station WZZK sponsors the sale of "Hope for Natalee" rubber-band bracelets. Jim and Nick's Barbeque and the local Blockbuster store get involved. Even little children sell lemonade for the neighbor girl who is lost. The Natalee Holloway Trust Fund is established to accept these contributions. It's managed by Regions Bank to make sure expenses are handled properly.

Amazingly, another very famous personality reaches out. Courtney Cox is from Birmingham and attended Mountain Brook High School. She and her husband, David Arquette, offer to sponsor a silent auction to raise money for the search. It's so humbling. Fund-raisers are under way from a band concert in Philadelphia, Pennsylvania, to another one in Pine Bluff, Arkan-

sas. We're going to need all the help we can get. We already do-
nated fifteen thousand dollars to Texas Equu-Search for their
expenses. The first stack of many attorney bills amounts to
$60,000. The medical evacuation plane that sat on the tarmac
here for three days when we thought Natalee was going to be
brought out of a crack house any minute cost $25,100. I'm a
speech pathologist. Natalee's father is an insurance agent. This
effort would have been abandoned weeks ago if not for the
caring and generous people who have stepped up to help. And
in the greatest show of unity and love, my fellow teachers come
forward one by one to donate vacation days so that I may continue to receive a paycheck while I stay here for Natalee. There's
no way I can ever thank everybody enough for these blessings. I
think everyone wants to see justice prevail.

Reporters and producers become our main source for encouragement and support here now. The tip line becomes the
media phone and is called the "Natalee line." They're staying on
this story. It must be making an impact back home, because I
continue to receive very thoughtful, detailed messages of hope as
well as continuous requests for TV, magazine, and newspaper
interviews. Even from television icon Barbara Walters. She sends
a letter asking me to call her. Sitting on a little stool in the dress-
ing area of the hotel room bathroom, I punch in her number.

"This is Natalee's mom. Barbara asked me to call. May I
speak with her?" Waiting for her to come to the phone, I see
myself in the mirror, phone to my ear, and think how strange it
is to be waiting for *Barbara Walters* to come to the phone.
Barbara, in her New York home. To talk to *me*, in Aruba. She

asks how I'm doing and is very sympathetic. Very nice. Encouraging. Complimentary of my actions on Natalee's behalf. The vote of confidence from her is uplifting. And she tells me that she has selected me to be on her annual list of the world's most fascinating people. It's so odd. I'm just looking for my daughter. Notoriety feels peculiar, but it's still truly an honor nonetheless.

"You've got my home number now if you need anything," she says. The conversation ends as surreal as it begins. And we hang up.

How interesting it is that being recognized and uplifted by family and friends, who love us no matter what, is one measure of hope. But when people with total objectivity, who don't have to love us no matter what, reach out to say, "You're doing the right thing. Stay the course," it has amazing influence. Add celebrity status to that and it's quite powerful. Barbara, Courtney, Brett, Kathie Lee, and so many others have great potential to bring comfort to people like me who are hurting. And it's so easy. A simple phone call or a simple note to remind us that we are all one. Schoolteachers or movie stars. No matter how famous—or infamous.

Joe Mammana is an anticrime crusader who bankrolls rewards for high-profile cases. A notorious past on the other side of the law gives him an interesting edge. He says he fully comprehends what we're dealing with here in Aruba as he offers a large sum for Natalee's reward. Joe calls daily to assess the situation and gradually increases the reward money from $50,000 to $250,000. It is split in two parts; a majority portion is made available for Natalee's safe return and a much smaller amount for information leading to her whereabouts. With this rapid succession in changing amounts we need new posters quite often. Jug's daughter, Megan, takes over this task for me. She designs a very professional-looking poster with Natalee's beautiful picture on it. The good people at Docu-pak, a marketing company near Birmingham, make thousands of these so that Megan can overnight them to us on the island. We have no way of knowing that after we receive the last batch indicating the highest amount to date, courtesy of Joe Mammana, they will soon become outdated. Again.

It's too expensive to use the hotel laundry service, so about once a week we go to a nearby coin laundry off the beaten path. It's in a third-worldly kind of neighborhood. Chickens, roosters, skinny mongrel dogs, and trash dot the yards around it. And we step over raw sewage, complete with soaked toilet paper, to get inside. But it's cheap and easy. Marilyn is here now, and as we fold our clothes, a call comes in.

It's the voice of a well-known American who has heard of our plight. Incredibly, he offers a one million dollar reward for Natalee's safe return. There are no strings attached. All we have to do is keep his name confidential. There is seemingly no end to the kind gestures of strangers, and I am so thankful for this. The flurry of offers of prayer, reward money, and seemingly everything else under the sun that people think might help us find Natalee, fill my days with hope and faith in mankind.

Megan goes back to work on new posters, this time creating them in three languages: English, Dutch, and Spanish. Everyone on the island should be able to read them: U. S. $1 million for Natalee's safe return and $250,000 for her whereabouts. Now surely, *surely*, someone will come forward. And the mere thought that a person believes so strongly that she could possibly be alive gives me great hope beyond explanation.

We've all seen tragedies in the news, but who among us actually calls to offer reward money or picks up a pen to craft a letter to someone who is suffering? The tone of the letters is changing. Where at first they contained prayers and scriptures, now the contents include pictures of families and pets, home phone numbers, cell phone numbers. It becomes very personal. People who were merely viewers of this crisis have become participants by reaching out to us. They send artwork created by their children to cheer me up. I am in awe of the empathy and begin to call them, thank them for their support, and ask if they have ever reached out like this before. The overwhelming majority say they have never done anything like this before.

Other angels in the outfield include people who have just shown up here to help out. Like Libby. She experienced a horrible tragedy in her life when her husband, two sons, and another relative drowned in a boating accident. She came right in and helped me get organized in the first couple of weeks. She does this good work through her DanPaul Foundation, named after the loved ones she lost. I am so grateful for her help, and for the outreach of so many.

Patrick is a man from the Cayman Islands who came to Aruba because he said he was "frustrated" over Natalee's case. He has a little girl. For six weeks he stayed on the island and went out on ground searches with Natalee's father, Dave. "I just wanted to help," he explained.

I believe people are taking action on our behalf because helping us through this nightmare gives them hope that someone would be there for them if they were in our shoes. When people help us feel better, they help themselves feel better too. Natalee's story is affecting people deeply. On a scale I could never have imagined until I saw it myself.

———————

THE FIRST BIG STEP in moving through this crisis was from hotel to hotel. The next is from land to land. With school starting soon, I want to go home to help my son, Matt, register and get ready for his junior year. Booking my return flight before I even leave gives me the courage to make the short trip home and depart the island for the first time in two months, the first time since landing here on Memorial Day. Natalee's father, Dave, and a host of other family members will remain here while I'm away. Knowing she's in good hands is the only way I can leave.

———————

I KNOW THE HOUSE will feel different before I even step inside. And it does. It's no longer warm and cozy. It simply doesn't feel the way home should feel. Not anymore. Macy the dog spends a lot of time in Natalee's room on the rug, still waiting. I spend a lot of time in here too. Seeing her bed that she hasn't slept in. Staring at her calendar, her plans for a great future, her scholarships. And the beautiful *Wizard of Oz* set she has never seen. All the promise lost. It makes me angry, and it makes me sick.

A neighbor who owns a clothing store lets me take Matt school shopping after closing time in privacy. It's great to spend this time with him. He is a man now. He became one very quickly this summer. And he's very supportive of my vigilance to see this through. "Don't give up, Mom. You *know* Natalee expects you to fight for her." And we laugh. Yes. Natalee always had high expectations.

In the store it's a strange feeling to see the fall clothes on the racks. For me, time is still. I'm stranded in this crisis on the island. Nothing moves forward there. But elsewhere, life progresses. And it's an odd realization.

After shopping for school clothes I stop in at a drugstore for some things. Standing in the checkout line I notice people to the left and right of me, staring at me. Waiting to pay the cashier, I look down to see the most shocking and outrageous thing I have ever seen in my life. Natalee is on the cover of a tabloid. Instantly I understand why the people around me are looking back and forth between the tabloid and me, and I feel like the freak in a sideshow. The one-eyed Cyclops carnival-goers pay to see. The words across the tabloid immediately make me feel abnormal. As if I don't fit into a civilized society anymore. I try not to look. It's all I can do to pay for the items and get out of the store. I'm embarrassed and devastated. But not nearly as hurt as I am after Matt tells me what happened to him at work.

My son bags groceries at the local grocery store. He says that he noticed the ghastly tabloids featuring his sister on the shelf near where he was working. They made him sick. Matt says the manager quietly went to the magazine area and removed all these despicable papers out of respect for him and for his family. I am very moved by the actions of this manager. Too bad there aren't people like this in every store everywhere, I think to myself. And in a flash I understand the vast impact of these rampant made-up stories: billions of people are reading these, and believing them, and we can't do anything about it. I'm helpless against the barrage of painful lies that appear in these articles. All I can do is look away. Powerless to do anything about it.

At home people bring food and drop notes in the mailbox. I wander into the kitchen and hear the TV. "Searchers today find no evidence in the case of missing Alabama teen Natalee Holloway …" And into the den, where another commentator says, "Today in the Natalee Holloway investigation …" And into the bedroom, where newspeople in different parts of the country are all discussing—even arguing—over Natalee's case. We do interviews on the island every day. But in my mind it never translated into this! It's nonstop coverage. We have become America's favorite reality TV show. I simply didn't know. In the grocery line, in schools and churches, at the proverbial watercooler everyone is talking about Natalee's case. I had no idea people were rushing home after work day after day to see if there was any news about her, eating their dinners in front of the TV so as not to miss anything. And now I understand the outpouring of love and support from all over the world.

Newspeople are debating the overwhelming and unprecedented interest in Natalee's case. Why is it so intense? Perpetual? What sets it apart from other missing-person cases, dominating TV news as well as the Internet? A number of Web sites have popped up just so people can log their comments and opinions, "blog," about the case on the Internet. Perhaps it's because all the elements of a real-life mystery are present. A beautiful graduate vanishes on an exotic trip with friends. Three suspects are known to be the last seen with her. The father of one is a prominent judicial official. A government duel ensues between the United States and Aruba on participation in the investigation. And viewers witness the clues as the case progresses, as we experience it, moment by moment, seeing all the signs that point in the same direction. Seeing for themselves the questionable circumstances in Aruba: the derailed investigation, outdated tactics, conflicting reports from government officials, contradicting stories from a myriad of potential witnesses and suspects, the lack of equipment and know-how, and the refusal of help from outsiders. Everyone is wondering why Aruba is more concerned about protecting the integrity of the three young men who were the last ones seen with Natalee than the reputation of their tiny island nation. I guess everyone just loves a good mystery. It's reality reality TV. And all this time I just didn't know.

———

JUG AND I WAIT UNTIL late at night after all the newspeople leave Mountain Brook Community Church to visit Natalee's Wall of Hope in private. Seeing it the first time is overpowering. Nine panels of wood, each about eight feet high and three or four feet across, and every square inch with a message written on it. Slowly, reverently, I run my fingers around the outline of the beautiful laser image of Natalee etched in marble. Her senior portrait, the centerpiece of the wall. I read the notes and the prayers and am stricken by the realization that Natalee is getting her messages of hope too. "We will never give up until we find you." "God loves you Natalee and so do we." "Please come home because your mom is crying," scribbles a child. Love from people everywhere. It's absolutely amazing. We stay more than an hour, light a candle for her, and promise to come back tomorrow for the prayer service. And again next month when the silent auction sponsored by Courtney Cox will take place.

All over town the yellow bows are fading to white, looking tattered, deteriorating in the summer heat. It's already time for Natalee's friends to go off to college and time for the last prayer service. It's a blessing to be here in prayer with them before they leave. Reverend Kallam invites Jug and me to the front of the service. I'm very emotional and unable to speak at first. Jug explains to the students that it's easy to sit and talk to strangers and state facts about the case to reporters and look into faceless camera lenses, but being with our loved ones and Natalee's friends is different. Powerful, and emotionally overwhelming. He thanks everyone and tells them how much their support has meant.

Finally finding the words, I explain to her friends how hard it was to make this trip, this first time leaving Natalee behind on the island. I tell them that it's good to take steps and that if I can do it, they can too. I want them to go in peace and be happy in their lives, not worry. They can pray for Natalee no matter where they live, because her spirit is everywhere. They have given so much love and worked so hard for her. It's time for them to move through this. So after hundreds of hugs and as many tears, some form of closure blesses these students tonight. And it's bitter-sweet.

"NATALEE'S MOM RETURNS FIGHTING MAD . . ." declare the networks when I get back to the island. Not mad. Just totally reenergized by the trip home, totally invigorated seeing all the incredible support for the first time, and determined to stay until the end. The deadline is looming, and the situation is urgent, as Joran covers his ears and refuses to cooperate with interrogators.

An MSNBC producer calls to tell me that Deepak is back on the job at the Internet café. I have some digital photos to print out and figure why not do it there? Sensing the need to document this, Marilyn, who has returned to the island with me, calls a network cameraman and tells him what I'm doing. He shows up with a small camera hidden in a plastic shopping bag, lens barely exposed, and sits down at one of the many computer stations. He pretends to type while aiming the camera at Deepak and me and videotapes the encounter.

Inside the store are rows of computers set up on long tables separated by aisles. The building is filled with people. Everyone is looking down at their keyboards, their backs to the aisles. No one sees me come in. Except Deepak. He's behind the cash register. I stop short of the counter and stand and stare at him for about fifteen minutes to gather my composure and get control of every emotion, to listen, look, assess. He keeps working. I know what I'm going to do. I approach the photo kiosk next to the counter and summon him.

"I need some help copying these digital shots, please." He comes from behind the counter and pins himself between the wall, the kiosk, and me. "Let's see … How do I print this?" As he shows me I ask, "Did you try to help her, Deepak? Or did you just watch?" There's no answer and I continue. "Can I crop this picture?" He shows me how. Then, "Did you watch while Joran put his finger in her? Did you do it too, Deepak?" He doesn't look up. Not once. I never see anything except the thinning spot on top of his head and continue to alternate between asking about the photos and about the night in question. "What color were her panties, Deepak? Green? Blue? Oh, yeah … they were green with dark blue embroidery, weren't they? Did they have a butterfly or was it a flower? It was a flower, wasn't it?" I ask and answer my own questions. Never raising my voice. Never losing control. And I'm finished.

Marilyn is waiting at the counter where I sling my purse up to get ready to pay. She asks, "Did you get two copies?"

"Oh no! I forgot," I say, and make my way back to the kiosk. "Oh, Deepak, we'll have to do it all over again."

He looks as if he could just dissolve into the floor, but reluctantly comes back over. The entire process is repeated, including the questions. And finally I ask him, "Do you want $250,000 in cash or life in prison? Look at me, please." His head is down. He goes back and forth between the counter and the kiosk during our encounter. He nervously flicks his pencil. He types senselessly on his keyboard.

I call him back over to the kiosk and this time repeat his own words to him from the statement he gave to police on June 13. The one that was read to us in the attorney general's office in which he tells how Paulus instructed the three young men to cover their tracks and get out of this mess they're in.

"Deepak, I *loved* the statement you gave to police at ten-thirty in the morning on June 13. Isn't that great the way Paulus helped you? Wow. You guys planned the whole thing. What to say. How to keep your stories straight and nail your alibi by e-mails ..."

And his head pops up.

He is shocked that I know this. My eyes blaze into his as I ask, "Don't you want the money, Deepak? Tell us what happened to Natalee."

He says only two things. "I don't need the money." Then, "The media have never seen this side of you."

To which I reply, "I was saving it for you, Deepak."

Sure enough, I receive a letter from Deepak's lawyer saying that I "threatened and harassed" him. The letter also states that if I go back to the Internet café, legal action will be taken against me. I never threatened Deepak. The video shot by the network cameraman proves that. As a result of this letter from Deepak's attorney, I had to officially respond by making a statement at the police station.

I stood up for Natalee again today. In the face of one of her perpetrators. And it felt good. Following the encounter Marilyn, the cameraman, and I meet up with the MSNBC producer, the one who tipped me off that Deepak was here, for lunch right next door to the Internet café. It's an open-air sandwich shop. The producer is enjoying a big salad when suddenly there is a spray coming down into the bowl. We all look up in time to see a giant iguana on a foliage-covered rafter above us. About the moment we realize what the spray really is, there's a plop! The little dinosaur defecates, and the droppings land right in the producer's bowl. Marilyn and I shriek! We all jump up, laughing hysterically. The embarrassed manager moves us to another table. The guys order something else. But no more food for the girls. No more appetite. And again I'm thankful that there are witnesses to this all too incredulous incident. You really can't make this stuff up.

Something else incredible happens today. My brother Paul and Carla, the wonderful New York PR person in charge of Aruba publicity, announce their engagement. Love blooms amid the crisis, and its beauty peeks out from behind the horror.

For Natalee

I don't like leaving Natalee here "alone." But as long as I know she is in good hands for a couple of days, I can make the second trip home. My friend Anola is a physician's assistant, Natalee's "doctor." She will return for a few days to serve as Natalee's parent on the island while I'm at home tending to personal matters and attending the silent auction that so many people have worked so hard on.

Long tables are lined with couture purses and guitars signed by famous rock and country stars. Beautiful jewelry glistens in the low lights. Autographed memorabilia from the *Friends* TV series attracts the interest of young and old patrons alike. All this makes me think how much Natalee would love to be here. This miraculous fund-raising event was put together so that we can continue to search for her. It's called simply *For Natalee*. And it's her down to every detail. The décor is all *Wizard of Oz*. And the shopping is fabulous. There just aren't words to express our gratitude for the $110,000 raised tonight at this benefit sponsored by Courtney Cox and David Arquette and organized by tireless friends in Mountain Brook. The only thing we know to do is stay strong. Keep up the fight for justice for Natalee. And make our community proud.

In all the noise and excitement I look down to see our new FBI agent calling my cell, snap back to reality as I know it, and run to the bathroom to answer it. "Beth. Bill. The Kalpoes are going to be rearrested in the morning." And again there is hope.

———————

SEVERAL SIGNIFICANT THINGS HAPPEN that appear to strengthen Natalee's case and lead to the Kalpoes' rearrest. Joran may have admitted sexual contact with Natalee with the Kalpoes present in the car. Therefore they are implicated. The gardener who says he saw the three suspects in Deepak's car near the pond at two-thirty on the morning that Natalee disappeared gives a sworn statement in front of a judge, the prosecution, the defense, and the three suspects. He swears that he saw Joran in the driver's seat, Deepak in the passenger's seat, and Satish in the back. The FBI is very encouraged by this witness, and his sworn statement is another reason the Kalpoes are rearrested. According to others present in the courtroom, Deepak appears very nervous when he hears the gardener's statement. He panics. And according to the FBI, contacts a young lady to ask her to lie for him. The young lady calls the FBI in the States and reports that Deepak asked her to give him an alibi for the night Natalee disappeared. They are trying to locate this girl. She says she "doesn't want to get involved" and doesn't leave her name. It's very hard to trace her number between international cell towers, but her information is riveting, and very, very important.

During this time we add a new attorney, Helen Lejuez, who tells us she is confident that she can access official documents for us. Her retainer is also $5,000 up front. We give her copies of all the materials we've collected. She gets started. And Vinda, the first attorney, quits, refusing to work on a team with Helen. Vinda sends another bill, for $15,000, but we are not able to obtain an itemized invoice for this.

All through August a good case seems to be building against the suspects. The FBI is optimistic. And the viewing public, vigilant via TV, is too. Evoking even more support, Dr. Phil invites me to appear on his show September 7 and sends a polygraph expert, Jamie Skeeters, to the island to offer the suspects the opportunity to participate in lie-detector tests.

Accompanying Jamie are two former FBI agents. They know a lot about this island and explain to us that Aruba is a "trampoline" country. "A Dutch military official is concerned that North Korean diplomats assigned to Cuba are laundering drug proceeds from South America in Aruba," one of the agents tells us. "The money is being used to finance North Korea's nuclear-arms program." The retired FBI agent says Secretary of State Condoleezza Rice has had meetings about this concern already. This is one very busy little island.

———————

EXCITED WITH THE NEWS that now all three suspects are in custody, friends Hal and Phillip accompany Jug and me back to Aruba after the auction. As we leave the mainland, a big hurricane is moving toward the United States. It's named Katrina. And our flight plan is altered to get around the storm.

It's Hal's first trip to Aruba, and his orientation in the bizarre begins right off the bat. Waiting for me at the hotel desk is an older man who wants some of Natalee's hair. He claims to have a divining-rod mechanism that will find her. So I give him a few strands out of her hairbrush. Thirty minutes later the older man calls and exclaims, "We got her!" The three men meet him out at the lighthouse, where he points to dense four-foot-thick lava rock and says with conviction, "She's in there." God love him. He flew here on his own dime and thought he could find her. But he'll need jackhammers and some TNT to get through that rock. Everyone wants the answer. And the reward too, I suppose.

Since June hundreds of psychics, visionaries, fortune-tellers, and other soothsayers have offered information, including incredibly detailed maps and drawings about what happened to Natalee. Others think they know where she is. "She's teaching school in a country called Aservia." "She is in the van der Sloots' freezer." (That one comes up a lot.) "I had a dream she's in a tank at the oil refinery." "A man in Curaçao is taking care of her." "Her body is in a container at the bottom of the ocean." "A woman is caring for her in an old house on the island." Of an average of sixty phone calls to log each day, about half are tips like these. Hal is astonished by all this. And his orientation is officially over.

Everyone seems to have a theory about what happened to Natalee. But as horrific as some of these mystic tips are, they don't even affect me anymore one way or the other. It's as if all that running back and forth and experiencing the sharp ups and downs on the emotional roller coaster have sort of evened out as the weeks pass on. I still cry when I'm sad. But don't have the outbursts. Don't throw things. And don't become alarmed anymore by anything anyone tells me. I can take the bullets to the gut and hold them now, keep them from exploding like little pellets all over my body. And release them on my time. When I'm ready.

Settling in for the night, we see and hear the first reports about that hurricane. It hit hard in Louisiana. Mississippi and Alabama are also affected. We all have loved ones at home in these states. The early reports of the devastation are unbelievable. News reporters are saying the death toll could exceed that of 9/11. Amazingly, media representatives on the island continue to call us and want to schedule interviews. But I decline. Our hearts ache for the people of New Orleans. Reports are telling us that this is the hardest-hit city. But visuals are not coming out yet of the most damaged areas. Reporters can't even get to those. We stand down from all our scheduled interviews and desperately await information on the aftermath of the giant hurricane.

SEPTEMBER 1 HELEN CALLS to say the court is asking for DNA from the Kalpoes and Joran van der Sloot and that their attorneys are fighting this. She also says the suspects are pointing the finger at one another. It's the Scarecrow scene all over again. Then she calls back and wants to know the name of Natalee's flip-flops. "They're called Rainbows, Helen." For the girl who loves Oz. Of course. But she doesn't say why they need this information. Do they have Natalee's shoes? Is this the evidence that will keep the three suspects in jail and bring justice? Helen is very positive. "It looks good that they will remain in custody," she says. Then just three hours after she tells me this encouraging news, a devastating call comes from an AP reporter.

"Paulus van der Sloot and his attorney are bragging to everyone that all three suspects are getting out day after tomorrow!"

Then all the media start calling. I call Helen, then FBI agent Bill and the U.S. vice-consul. None of them have this information. So we tell the media it must be a rumor. But the word is out all over the island from the defense side that all three suspects will walk.

Four and a half hours after this announcement is made to international media by Joran's father and his defense team, the FBI calls to tell me it is indeed true. So the three suspects who were last seen with my daughter, and who offered multiple versions of what happened that night, will go free. And we are the last ones to find out.

Natalee's handwriting on her immigration card states that the duration of her stay here would be four nights. It has been ninety-five. And I have painstakingly counted every one of them.

When Helen calls, I stand in a corner of the hotel room, phone to my ear, tapping my head against the wall over and over. Tears fall hard. "I'm done, Helen. I'm done. No justice for Natalee in Aruba. I'm done."

Shortly after this phone conversation the hotel housekeeper comes in to deliver towels. She's a beautiful Aruban woman about my age. She takes my hand and pulls me to the floor with her. We are on our knees. With my hand in hers, she raises our arms together. We are outstretched. Then she lowers us down, chests to the floor, still on our knees, then raises us up again. She takes me with her. Down, then up. Our arms high in praise. She looks upward, and in broken English cries out, "Please, God, help this lady! Help this lady! Please! Please, God!" We cry together. And I realize she already knew the suspects were getting out. *The maid already knew.*

DOWNSTAIRS THE STRATEGIC COMMUNICATIONS Task Force is holding a media meeting to give instructions for Saturday's release. "There will be an imaginary line around the van der Sloot home. If you cross it you will be deported," they sternly warn the reporters. Then producers learn that their broadcast licenses will not be renewed. What they paid $400 for in June now costs their networks three and four times that, according to one CNN producer. "They're making it up as they go," the producer says. And he continues by telling me that a member of the task force is leaving yelling, cursing, blistering messages on his cell phone about the news coverage. The island is finished. Shutting us out. Sending our demand for justice home.

The Dutch interrogators, who have tried as hard as the FBI to help us, come up to the room. They are trying to make heads or tails of this. "In Holland this never would have happened," one of them tells me. "The defense is running the show." They were as shocked as we were that the three will be released and said information was presented to the judge that showed ample reason to keep them in custody.

As we talk, calls come in from reporters that prosecutor Karin Janssen is in a mud pit in her high heels with a search team. Attorney Helen says it's because one of the boys is talking. That's absolutely crazy. They walk soon. Why talk now?

Then FBI agent Bill comes by and delivers the final blow. "The FBI has never received one single document from the Arubans. Not one tape. Nothing," he says sadly. Despite our personal pleas to authorities here and our broadcast appeals to Aruba to let the FBI lend a hand, and regardless of Aruba's public response that it would welcome FBI assistance, the island never let FBI agents in on the investigation. Never passed them the ball. Not even for one minute. And Bill explains how the release of the three suspects happened. "The information the FBI was given was that the judge gave Joran thirty more days, up to October 1. And he gave the Kalpoes eight more days. But then the judge flew back to Curaçao and faxed a reverse decision from there." The reverse decision decreed that all three will go free.

The opportunity to hide behind Hurricane Katrina is too inviting. The three suspects will be released while all eyes are turned to the devastation in New Orleans. And the island shutdown begins.

The tide of support turns further away from Natalee and her family, and I'm not comfortable here anymore. Dr. Phil offers to take us out of here tomorrow. We go to our regular nearby coin laundry to get ready and are confronted there by two henchmen. A man with light hair, blistering blue eyes, and profound acne scarring approaches my friend.

"Are you Natalee's mom?" he asks her.

"No. She's outside."

I'm in the car on the phone waiting for her to bring the clothes out. A car pulls up very close to my driver's door, pinning me in. The man motions for me to put my window down.

"When are you leaving?" he asks. "You look very tired. And you're getting kind of skinny. Is it time to go home?"

We load up the clothes and realize what just happened.

The island authorities originally planned to release the three suspects at two o'clock in the morning on Saturday, September 3. The Strategic Communications Task Force undoubtedly helped them make a less conspicuous move and release them in the afternoon instead. Curious to see the setup at the van der Sloot house for Joran's parade of victory, I drive by there, never in a million years expecting to see who is there. It's the U.S. vice-consul. At the van der Sloots' house. Why is she here? She spots me. Jumps in her car and follows me to a restaurant parking lot, waving, honking, calling on the cell phone. I don't want to talk to her. Who can we trust? We go inside the restaurant and a minute or two later in walks "Scarface," the goon from the laundry yesterday. We're being followed. And it's getting rougher here by the minute.

The last announcement I make on television is never seen. Hurricane Katrina gives the island the cloak of cover it needs to let the suspects walk free and relieve itself of its media burden. In the final press statement I remind anyone listening that there is still a $1 million reward for Natalee's safe return and $250,000 for her whereabouts. And I pledge to be her voice for the rest of my life, to take up this cause from the home front. All parents would want the same justice for their child.

As happened before, everyone in the room becomes emotional. Reporters, camerapeople, and producers are like our brothers and sisters now. After spending three months working closely together on Natalee's case, we don't want to leave it this way on such a low note. So in a final show of support from media comrades we gather for a "Dutch treat" dinner at a nearby restaurant. And in unprecedented unity more than twenty-five media professionals from all different networks from all over the world sit down at a table together. For Natalee. And we say our good-byes. The only one who apparently doesn't understand what "Dutch treat" means is from London. She leaves her check. So we pay it.

Remarkably, just before the three suspects walk free, one of the most popular island tourist attractions, the coral rock Natural Bridge, collapses into the sea. And with one last powerful proverbial sign from the heavens, it's over.

"ARE YOU LEAVING FOR GOOD NOW?" a member of the Strategic Communications Task Force asks as I'm on the way to the airport. Then the rental-car company calls and wants its car back. After we paid for the first month's rental, it offered the car free for the past two months, which we greatly appreciated. "I'm bringing it to you right now, okay?" As soon as I leave, the prime minister releases a statement encouraging his citizens to turn their attention to the island's economic growth.

It takes thirteen hours to travel from Aruba to Hollywood, California, to the *Dr. Phil* show. The farther away from the island we get, the more panic tries to raise its ugly head and has to be fended off. Can't watch the movie. Can't talk much. Just trying to maintain composure after yesterday's trauma. And wondering what will become of Natalee's case now.

Aruban authorities never took statements from the Alabama men, the eyewitnesses who were present at the van der Sloots' that first morning. And no statement was taken from that DEA agent. Aruba simply wouldn't do it. We had to do it. So after the suspects were released, the coach, Mat, and Ruffner took it upon themselves to give sworn statements before a U.S. district judge in Alabama so that their testimony about what Joran said he did to Natalee would be officially recorded.

After waiting months to find out what my statement actually says, Jug calls on my first day in California. He has finally been able to obtain the translation of my statement from prosecutor Karin Janssen. The one the detective brought to me to sign late that night in the restaurant. The same night he told the men not to disturb the crack houses and whorehouses. And I trusted him, and signed every page. "Listen to this, Beth ..." The words he reads echo in my head. I begin to sink, and could slide to the ground out of my chair.

"Jug, they changed it. They changed my statement." I had carefully given intricate details about the encounter in the van der Sloot front yard the first night we got to the island, including names and physical descriptions. Now Paulus van der Sloot is described only as "the man with the glasses." Those are not my words.

Earlier we learned from the prosecutor that the statements from the two uniformed officers who were with us in the van der Sloot front yard that morning don't mention the sexual encounters described by Joran between Natalee and him. No mention of his sexual contact with her as she was falling asleep and waking up. No mention of his description of her underwear and genitalia. So the judge never heard about all that. There's no way a police officer could stand there that morning, hear what Joran was saying, and fail to include these details in a statement. No way. In my opinion this information must have been deleted *for* the officers.

And no, Natalee, we're not in Kansas anymore.

————————

WE'VE PLAYED BY THE RULES. I kept confidences when asked to and have not revealed the statements that were read to all of us that day in the attorney general's office. But I'm finished now. A long time ago Jug and I decided that if the suspects walk, we talk. It's time to disclose what we know, so the world can hear the words of the suspects and fully understand why we had to stay on this like we have. And fight.

Checking with agent Bill, I get the all-clear. "You can say whatever you want, Beth. No rules. No secrets. Not anymore." So on the *Dr. Phil* show I tell what Joran said on June 9 about his encounter with Natalee—sexually explicit and graphically detailed. I tell what Deepak said on June 13 about getting guidance from Paulus. I tell about my statement being changed.

Dr. Phil is outraged and unexpectedly calls for a boycott of the island of Aruba.

All the way back to Aruba after the *Dr. Phil* show I think about having to leave the island now. It's useless to stay there. We fought honestly and fairly and gave it our best shot. But we have lost the battle. It's the proverbial, biblical conflict between good and evil. It's very, very hard to fight evil because it constantly changes form and you never know who your enemies are. And evil is always two steps ahead. From the outset we never had a chance. But we didn't know it. If we had known all our efforts would be futile, perhaps we wouldn't have been so compelled to work this hard. I feel as though I have failed those who have stood with us because we weren't successful in bringing Natalee home. But I don't believe I have failed Natalee. I have done everything in the world I could possibly think of on her behalf, everything any parent would have done. All possibilities have been exhausted. And I have no regrets. I'll continue to work for justice for Natalee from the home front. I'm taking leave of the island, but not from the work yet to be done.

Jug, his daughter, Megan, and friends Heather and Phillip come to Aruba to help pack and take me home. Our actions are mechanical as we close down Natalee's command post in the Wyndham hotel room. Thousands of pages of documents, newspaper articles, press releases, notes, letters, and a trunk full of treasures from caring people are all packed up. Everything is packed except for a large bundle of letters I keep aside to read on the plane ride home.

Downstairs we pay the $19,000 hotel bill. And leave Aruba.

The Boycott

Communications continue to deteriorate between the family and authorities in Aruba. In an attempt to improve the situation, attorney Helen schedules an October meeting for me with prosecutor Karin Janssen and chief deputy Gerold Dompig. Concerned about my accusations on the *Dr. Phil* show that my statement was altered, they offer me the chance to give another one. I welcome the opportunity to do that as well as to hand deliver a letter to Aruban officials outlining all our concerns about Natalee's case and asking that the prosecutorial and investigative teams be replaced.

The date is set. Flight and meeting times are set. But the night before I am to leave for this mid-October meeting on the island, attorney Helen calls with a desperate warning not to come.

"Actions will be taken against you. You could be arrested," she says and asks me not to say that she called to warn me that if I go there I may not be allowed to leave.

"Well, Helen, when the media ask me why I'm not coming, I have no choice but to tell them I'm being threatened."

She begs me not to tell. "If you say I told you about this, I will have to move there and rent a bedroom from you."

The dark influence. It's so apparent. She is scared of something. Or someone.

The Strategic Communications Task Force wastes no time releasing a statement suggesting I stood them up. Their report states: "Janssen and Dompig did schedule a meeting to take place. However, Beth changed her flight, missed the meeting, and did not even call to cancel or reschedule."

Immediately I want to clear the air about this and try to set up another meeting date. I offer to give a new statement. But chief deputy Dompig won't return calls now. Neither will the prosecutor. I get word from attorney Helen that if I agree to answer questions about fund-raising, then perhaps I can have a meeting with Dompig *if he approves of my answers to these questions.* I have to jump through some hoops to get a meeting with the police. As crazy as it sounds, I agree to do this.

On November 1, in the middle of an uncharacteristic monsoon of a rainstorm, my brother Paul, friend Carol, and I arrive in Aruba for meetings. When I sit down with detective Jacobs to what I believe will be an opportunity to give a new statement, I find instead I'm being interrogated! The Arubans want to know about *my* ties to Venezuelan and Columbian money! They want to know about the fund-raising in the United States. They accuse me of setting up Natalee's disappearance to scam the public and raise millions of dollars. Anyone who wants to do the math can plainly see that nowhere near a million dollars was raised. Then they blame her disappearance on the other Mountain Brook students, saying they intend to go to Alabama to interrogate them, even though the FBI has already offered to share all of the students' statements with the Arubans. Eventually some Aruban officials suggest on the air that Natalee ran away. That she died of a drug overdose. That she was selling drugs on the island. Apparently their new strategy is to blame the victim. And her family.

When it's all over, the meeting with Dompig never materializes. However, he does appear on Rita Cosby's MSNBC program on November 2. During the course of the interview Rita asks him, "Do you believe, chief—you said to me even before this interview that you believe the boys are guilty as hell. Do you believe they're involved in her disappearance?" And Dompig replies simply, "Yes."

Attorney Helen hands me a typed letter from the prosecutor stating that she doesn't have time in her schedule to meet with me. After I leave Aruba, it's reported on the island that Dompig and Janssen *did* meet with me. And that's not true.

However, there is one opportunity to communicate with some island officials. A group of concerned hoteliers and other businesspeople wants to discuss the tone of the *Dr. Phil* show and his call for a boycott and invites me to attend their meeting. Paul and Carol go with me. We show this group the letter we brought to give to authorities outlining all the barriers we have faced since Natalee disappeared, all the bungled police work in the first ten days, and all the lost evidence. As they peruse it, some of them appear to be surprised at the problems we've had along the way. In addition, we explain that the only thing Tim Miller and his Texas Equu-Search teams needed recently was for the Aruban authorities to call the FBI to officially request, as in invite, the deep-water search equipment. Tim had everything lined up and was all set to start searching the ocean. All the officials had to do was make the call to satisfy protocol. When they refused to make that one simple phone call, Tim became frustrated and pulled his teams from the island.

For these reasons and many others, we request in the letter to authorities that the investigative and prosecutorial teams be replaced. "We've always been concerned about the relationship between police chief van der Straten and the prime suspect's father, Paulus van der Sloot," my brother explains. "It was never our intent to hurt Aruba or the Aruban people in any way, but there's an appearance of collusion." Several members of the task force nod in agreement.

It's quiet in the room when I add, "Oh, come on. Everyone knows there was a cover-up."

And to this, Jorge Pesquera, president and CEO of the Aruba Hotel and Tourism Association, shrugs his shoulders, nods in the affirmative, and says softly, "Yes ... yes there was."

A GOOD-HEARTED, WELL-MEANING legislator in Alabama introduced a resolution back in July to boycott Aruba. We contacted him directly then and asked him not to move forward with that. We thanked him for his dedication to Natalee, but explained that we were trying to give the Aruban justice system a chance to work. We were committed to playing by Aruba's rules, strange as they were to us. We kept thinking, just let it work. We aren't at home. They have their own ways of doing things. Patience. Patience. But no more. We are completely shut out. Alabama governor Bob Riley is shut out. Aruba isn't taking his calls or anyone else's. The last straw comes when the Alabama governor receives a letter in November from the director of the Department of Foreign Affairs in Aruba stating that "the Chief Prosecutor leading the investigation and the General Prosecutor are appointed by the Kingdom Government in The Hague ... and because of separation of powers the Government of Aruba has no authority to intervene in the investigation." *The government of Aruba has no authority to intervene?*

For five months we ran around in circles on the island begging for help, trying to get answers about who is in charge. No one ever mentioned The Hague. No one pointed us in the right direction. Not the prime minister, not the minister of justice, not the attorneys to whom we've paid tens of thousand of dollars. No one. They just watched us suffer.

Our last-ditch effort to get Aruba's attention is a boycott. And we do not come to this in haste. Governor Riley signs the bill, saying he believes we have been patient with Aruba to a fault. Georgia governor Sonny Purdue and Arkansas governor Mike Huckabee follow suit. U.S. senator Richard Shelby sends letters to other politicians asking for their support of the boycott. And despite claims from Aruba that it only created a blip on their tourism radar, the number of visitors to that island has been reduced. Reportedly "dismal." Either due to the boycott or the case itself or both.

In a final attempt to reestablish communications and find resolution in Natalee's case, the family retains celebrated international lawyer John Q. Kelly. It's a great relief when he takes over the case. Soon he helps us file a civil suit against Joran van der Sloot. It cost $130,000 to have investigators and attorneys from here to Scotland Yard serve papers on Joran the moment he landed on U.S. soil in New York. He came here for TV interviews.

Still, there is no answer. And almost no money left to fight for justice for Natalee.

We've been in communication with everyone from Secretary of State Condoleezza Rice to Dog the Bounty Hunter trying to get help. In Birmingham to attend a Sunday service where Secretary Rice's father used to preach, I have the extraordinary honor of sitting down with her for a few minutes. Entering her hotel suite, I am led to my seat. The most powerful woman in the world enters, and I can actually feel it as I approach her to shake hands.

She sits down across a coffee table from me. Behind her are two official-looking men. I start talking a hundred miles a minute, because I know my time with her is limited and I want to get it all in. I tell her about Natalee's case and about everything that went wrong from the first night we arrived on the island. How suspicious the events surrounding the investigation have been. I tell her what I've learned about money laundering in Aruba to support the North Korean nuclear-arms program and about the drugs there. She is very attentive. I continue talking very fast, seated on the edge of my chair, and conclude by asking her for assistance from the FBI. Real assistance. I ask her if there is anything she can do to get Aruba to let the Bureau help in Natalee's case. She speaks once. She turns to the two men behind her and says, "I want the FBI back on this." And that's all. I thank her, and I know how lucky I am to have had this private meeting with Secretary Rice and what a privilege it is. I pray that whatever happens in Natalee's favor as a result of this meeting will one day help others who may find themselves in our family's desperate predicament.

It's a very sad realization that there's really nothing anyone or any amount of money can do for us. One would think that a reward for $1 million for Natalee's safe return and even $250,000 for her whereabouts would be enough to obtain information. But it isn't. Why is that? The answer is that the information about what happened to Natalee simply isn't for sale. Most native Aruban citizens have never left the island. If they were to snitch and tell on someone, they would certainly have to leave there. What good is all that money with no island? No home? There is apparently no amount of money in the world that can get us the answer to what happened to Natalee. When I asked an Aruban attorney about this, his response was chilling: "The threat is bigger than the money," he says. *The threat*. That dark influence. The evil that nothing and no one can pierce.

THE DINING ROOM IN OUR HOUSE is transformed into Natalee's new command post as well as my new sanctuary, replacing the Alto Vista chapel as a place for prayer and reflection. The holidays will be here soon, and we'll have to face the first season without Natalee. In Mountain Brook the yellow bows are removed from mailboxes and fence posts and collected at City Hall. People who bring in their bows sign a pledge to continue supporting us through prayer. It's time to make room for holiday decorations on mailboxes and storefronts around town. Beautiful magnolia arrangements trade places with the yellow bows. And it's a poignant irony that one symbol of hope is replaced by another. People ask what I will do, how we'll get through it. But it's not the holidays and birthdays that get to me. It's the milestones. Natalee would be looking forward to her winter break after her first semester at college. But she isn't coming home from college for Christmas. She isn't coming home.

The articles and letters and treasures are stacked high in the dining room. There's almost no floor space left. After close to five months, I find that I don't need to suit up with these tangible symbols of faith as much anymore. As my heart tries to begin to understand the loss, I become more sure-footed. Little by little there is less need for ritualistic actions. Less need for outward signs, as I rely on the evidence of things *not* seen. And just like during the epiphany at the Stations of the Cross, I understand again that the mind can't comprehend what the heart has to endure.

In this room the things that collected here while I was gone merge with the items brought back from Aruba, and every day is like a treasure hunt. New things are discovered every time I sit down on the floor in here to look around. I can stay in here all day and night and still not see everything. Beautiful cards. Drawings. Scriptures. There are a half dozen CDs with music written about Natalee. And meaningful poems.

I spend days on end organizing and reorganizing all the items. And ponder what is next, now that my work in Aruba has ended. I'm so thankful that John Kelly has taken on Natalee's case. I'm relieved of worrying about the investigative matters with him at the helm. Many suggest I go back to teaching. But my precious students require 110 percent from me every day. And I don't have that to give. Not yet.

Other people close to me delicately propose therapy. "Just talk to someone. A professional," loved ones advise. This opportunity presents itself through Libby, the woman who showed up on the island in the early days to help us get organized. She invites me to join her at a retreat in New Mexico. It's a grief therapy facility. The one she went to after she lost her family in a tragic boating accident.

We spend five days there. It's a beautiful and peaceful place, and the emotional and spiritual cleansing it advocates is centered around meditation and getting in touch with your inner spirit. I find it to be very healing. Uplifting. And I am grateful that she shared this place and this experience with me.

What has helped me the most is what I call "retail therapy." Shopping makes me happy. I don't know if it's because it takes my mind off everything or because it makes me feel close to Natalee. This was our thing we did together almost every Saturday morning. Maybe I still think I might catch a glimpse of her across the clothing racks or see her sitting at the makeup counter. I don't buy something all the time. Just shop. Just touch the fabrics and feel the different environment. It's an escape. And comforting to my senses. The experience stimulates good feelings.

Happy memories. This self-imposed therapeutic treatment goes on for several months until I no longer need it.

Natalee's bright green sequined Dorians uniform hangs here in the dining room among all the treasures. It looks so small. Dainty. Staring at it long and hard, I think about the girl who dreamed all her life of being on the dance team. And made it. Leg injury and all. About the young lady who worked so hard to succeed at everything she did. The same young woman who got the university scholarships. My child. My beautiful daughter. I can't save her. It's too late. Natalee is gone. And second to the great tragedy of losing her is if we fail to learn from what has happened.

I could be any parent in the world. And no parent should ever go through this experience. Natalee could be anyone's daughter. And in these thoughts a new path is made clear. There *is* something I can do. Many people reached out to us, and I can now reach back to them. It might be too late to save Natalee, but it's not too late to save others. And it's time now to make good on my pledge to stand before high-school and college students, law enforcement professionals, victims' rights groups, travelers of all ages, and anyone interested in personal safety to share Natalee's story and our hard lessons, so that others might learn from them. The program is named the Safe Travels safety awareness campaign, because that's what travelers say to one another to wish each other a safe journey. This is my tribute. And hope is again transformed. From the need to find Natalee, to the need for an answer, to the need to help keep others from going through our experience.

Another way to give back some of what was given to us is by reaching out to parents of other missing children. In Orlando,

Florida, a mother and father are distraught over the disappearance of their college-age daughter several months ago. I call them, and send them some teas in a gift basket with a letter, taking what I learned from so many others and using it to pass along the peace that hope brings.

A high-school teacher, a local beauty pageant queen, is missing in Ocilla, Georgia. I go there, meet with the missing woman's family, and talk to them about things they can do to help investigators, help themselves, and keep moving forward. Tim Miller and Texas Equu-Search are on site too. And for the first time I see Tim in his element. He has an extraordinarily advanced high-tech command-post bus at his disposal, made possible by Homeland Security funds for this Georgia county. He has drone planes and is using them to map search grids. There are laptops and maps and all kinds of communications equipment. In Aruba, Tim and his team were not even provided maps by the authorities. Some of his equipment was not allowed into the country. And in the end he was unable to even have a simple phone call made to allow the FBI to bring in their deep-water equipment—which was on standby, ready and waiting. Tim was trying to do his job on the island with both hands and one leg tied. But here I see what could have been. I see his capabilities and rejoice that the family of this missing schoolteacher have all these resources available to them.

And I thank God that I live in a country where human rights are valued and justice for all is expected.

Lessons

The remains of pregnant twenty-four-year-old Latoyia Figueroa, the mother of a seven-year-old girl, were found one month after she disappeared near Philadelphia, Pennsylvania. Her boyfriend is charged with her death and the death of her unborn child. Latoyia's father, Melvin Figueroa, is the first victim's parent I meet as we participate together in a missing persons conference sponsored by the Philadelphia City Council. Melvin is an intensely spiritual man of great faith, warm and inviting. We embrace when we meet and share tears together over the loss of our daughters. It's easy to see that he was a very devoted father to Latoyia. We talk about our girls. And cry. And I gather great strength from him.

Joe Mammana made it possible for me to receive an invitation to this conference in Philadelphia, where parents of missing loved ones or those who are victims of violent crime can share our stories and learn from one another. Following this meeting, Joe also makes it possible for me to present the very first Safe Travels

message at the Columbus, Ohio, high school Julie Popovich attended. Julie went missing after getting into a car with a man her
friends did not recognize. She was found murdered.

To prepare for this presentation, I carefully reconsider the
lessons learned in Aruba and come to three main conclusions.
First, young adults in the transitional age group between high
school and college need their own specific message about personal safety. They need to be reminded, in their own language,
of the lessons their parents taught them about life's dangers, including not getting into a situation or condition in which they
can't choose their free will.

Second, safety plans have to come full circle, because young
adults' personal safety is their own responsibility now, and they've
got to have "their own back."

And third, travelers need to take better preparedness measures before leaving the United States, which includes gathering
specific destination information such as police precinct numbers, attorney names, and other data that is not currently available. This is needed because once you get to your destination,
this information may not be readily accessible (as in our case).
Tips like activating international calling and securing a temporary medical evacuation plan before leaving are critical and must
also be included.

––––––––––

WITH THIS INITIAL OUTLINE, the first Safe Travels presentation is
made in Ohio.

On this day the high-school seniors are excused at noon. The
principal is concerned that many won't return for the safety pre-

sentation. But they do. And nearly eight hundred young adults fill the gymnasium. The message begins with a wonderful tribute to Natalee, a DVD created by friends Ellen and Jim. Photos of Natalee with her friends, on the dance team, at graduation, and in other scenes are all set to a beautiful and insightful song composed by Christian music songwriter Ericka Harvey from Nashville. The visuals project onto a large screen as Ericka sings, "Every time my heart beats I want to cry … Natalee, where are you now?" And the giant room falls silent.

Following the DVD, I step up to the podium. Photos of Natalee appear behind me on a power point as I tell her story to the students. How she was on top of the world when she left on her senior trip to Aruba. How she had graduated from high school and was on her way to college. She was savvy, and I was confident that I had taught her all the things she needed to know about the world around her. Then I explain that on the last day of her trip she failed to show up for her flight home. And we learned that she had disappeared in the company of three young men who live on the island. "Natalee was blindsided and never stood a chance against her perpetrators," I tell them.

The students are very attentive as I explain that Natalee had a false sense of security there among her many friends. She must have felt that being in Carlos 'n Charlie's with a big group made her safe. She was too confident. She felt *too* safe. She let her guard down for a moment, and in that moment she vanished.

In our American society we're surrounded by the faces of missing people. They're on milk cartons, billboards, posters, and mail flyers and continue to be the topic of nightly news shows. I tell these students: "You're at the age where your parents have loosened the reins. You're breaking out on your own, excited about your newfound independence. And somewhat caught between that healthy fear of danger your parents taught you, and complacency. You're too old to be guarded by your mom and dad, and too young *not* to be reminded that there are dangerous people and dangerous places in the world."

The best thing I can ask these students to do is protect themselves by initiating a full-circle safety plan—no matter where they are.

"*You* are responsible for your own safety now. Your parents aren't going to be around anymore to watch over you," I tell them, explaining that once Natalee got into that car she was at the mercy of her perpetrators and could no longer protect herself.

"Your safety plan must come full circle. You must pay as much attention to how you plan to end your evenings as you spend deciding what you're going to wear and who you're going out with. A full-circle safety plan is something you have to take responsibility for."

What if Natalee had made a plan with her friends that they would all leave together at the end of the night? What if she and a friend had set a time and place to meet before they left the establishment? What if . . .

The group remains remarkably attentive and respectful as I make clear that, even though they are on the threshold of adulthood, they must always remember the safety rules their parents taught them: "Never go anywhere alone. Don't leave a place with someone you don't really know. Don't leave your beverage unattended, and don't get into a situation or a condition where you can't make good decisions or choose your free will. If you feel uncomfortable about a situation, get away from it. Go with your gut feeling. Be aware of what's going on around you."

I tell them that I applaud their plans to travel and study abroad and encourage them to take advantage of these opportunities. I just want them to be sure they understand that when they leave the United States there are consequences and challenges to face if something tragic happens. They must understand that the rules are different in other countries and help is not as readily available as it is here. So they must be careful and be prepared before they leave. They are their own best protection, whether traveling to the mall or traveling outside the United States.

At the conclusion of this presentation the students give a standing ovation. Not just for Natalee, but for Latoyia and Julie and all the other victims of violent crime. The principal says he has never seen his students react this way. And again I am persuaded by the encouragement of others to stay the course. Nudged to move forward with this campaign.

Soon after this presentation, the president of the National Sheriffs' Association, Sheriff Ted Sexton, of Tuscaloosa County, Alabama, invites me to speak at their annual conference in Palm Springs. The NSA is the largest law enforcement organization in the country, and I am humbled and honored to accept the invitation. I carry the same message to the sheriffs that I delivered at the high school in Ohio, adding that I want to be able to give every student a little decal for their rearview mirror that says Safe Travels, so that every time they look up to see what's behind them, they're reminded that they've got their own back. The message is very well received, and the executive committee of the NSA passes a resolution to endorse the Safe Travels safety campaign. Sheriff James Arnold from Indiana offers to pay for the first one thousand decals. And the mission is officially under way.

At the NSA conference I have the privilege of meeting Dr. Charles Steele, president and CEO of the Southern Christian Leadership Conference. The SCLC has been at the forefront of the human rights movement, advocating peace and justice worldwide, since its inception in 1957. It was founded under the leadership of Dr. Martin Luther King Jr.

Dr. Steele invites me to meet with him at the SCLC headquarters in Atlanta to discuss how they might help open communications with Aruba and potentially negotiate a resolution regarding Natalee's case. In his conference room is a very long, old, scratched-up table. It takes up the whole room. "This was Dr. King's table," he says. When we sit, I lay my palms flat out on it and run my hands toward the center. It's a spiritual moment, as I think about the words that have been spoken around this table for human rights, civil rights, peace, and justice. The SCLC offers to act on Natalee's behalf and sends letters to the prime minister of Aruba, the prosecutor, police chief deputy Dompig, former police chief van der Straten, the minister of justice, and the minister of tourism requesting meetings. The SCLC is prepared to go to Aruba for Natalee, because as

Dr. Steele says, in Dr. King's words, "Injustice anywhere is a threat to justice everywhere." But Aruban authorities never respond to Dr. Steele's letters or phone calls.

The National Sheriffs' Association conference is the launch pad for the nationwide Safe Travels safety campaign and the birthplace for the International Safe Travels Foundation (ISTF). From here I begin to make my way around the country to speak to schools, churches, law enforcement organizations, attorney generals' conferences, and victims' rights conferences. As a result, two goals come into view that I believe will help the millions of Americans who travel internationally every year have a safer trip. The goals are education and a reexamination of the emergency assistance procedures for American victims in crisis in a foreign country.

The goal of education is twofold: to bring a message about personal safety to high-school and college students and to educate travelers. Many students, families, and travelers of all ages are planning fabulous international trips. The Safe Travels message is *not* about discouraging international travel. But in today's world we are remiss if we fail to address personal safety at a much higher level than in the past. It's about so much more than telling church missions participants to stay with their group or high-school students to watch their drinks.

Bad things happen everywhere. But the difference we need to consider when something bad happens outside the country is *the help available* for the victims and their families. When we leave these borders, we leave behind all the privileges and rights we're all accustomed to and often take for granted. We have

expectations that there will be a safety net of law-abiding officials, no matter where we travel, or that our U.S. embassy will
come to our rescue. But that's terribly naive. Our U.S. constitu-
tional rights don't apply in other countries. Once you leave here
you are absolutely on your own. I can testify to that. But if we
educate travelers by making more in-depth information about
their destination available to them, offer preparedness measures
they should take before they leave home, and take a second look
at the victims' assistance that is supposed to be in place, then I
believe people will have safer international travel experiences.
And perhaps lives could be saved.

In a world that is becoming increasingly unstable, travel-
safety education is vital to the security of international travelers,
especially Americans. When I got the call that a donor is making
the International Safe Travels Foundation curriculum–based
study a reality at prestigious Auburn University in Alabama, I
silently congratulated Natalee: *You're doing good work, girl.*
Dr. Martin O'Neill and Dr. Susan Hubbard in the College of
Human Sciences are overseeing the research for the ISTF study
at Auburn. The facilitator of the ISTF study is graduate student
Lindsay Waits. She is enthusiastic about her findings thus far,
and has been very successful delving into the issues of travel
safety to help educate students and all travelers, as well as make
critical information available on a Web site. My vision to create
a one-stop-shop Web site where travelers can investigate their
destinations to prepare for safer trips is coming to life at www.
safetravelsfoundation.org. By clicking on the next generation
map, visitors can pull up their destination and gather and print

important data to take with them. This Web site is in its infancy, and my prayer is that the Safe Travels university study will continue to be funded so that the information available on the Web site for travelers can continue to expand. The first year of the Auburn study is made possible by the DanPaul Foundation, which was established by my friend Libby, the woman who came to the island to help me in the early days of Natalee's disappearance, the one who took me to the therapeutic retreat in New Mexico.

Early results of the study are already remarkable. In a pretest, students almost always reply that they believe the U.S. embassy will come to their rescue and handle whatever crisis they might get into—and pay for all their legal and other related expenses as well! The powers of the embassy are limited as to the amount of assistance it can provide.

The curriculum-based International Safe Travels study focuses on travel-safety education and the measures that travelers should take when faced with crises while abroad. The study addresses customs, police and law enforcement, contact information at police precincts, medical facilities, safe and dangerous places within destinations, alcohol and drug laws, and many, many other areas that will result in valuable and pertinent information for travelers.

Following education, the second goal to help American international travelers is more long-term: a reexamination of current traveler-assistance procedures. When crimes are committed, the response time is critical. Could Natalee have been found if there had been some kind of cooperation between U.S. and

Aruban law enforcement? I can't answer that. But I do wonder about it. What if that Homeland Security representative or that DEA agent we met on the island that first night could have intervened on our behalf in some way? What if we could have met the U.S. vice-consul before the fifth day after Natalee's disappearance? And of course, I feel certain we would have an answer today had the FBI actually been allowed to participate in the investigation. But we'll never know.

American travelers put a lot of trust in the U.S. embassy when they get into a situation outside this country. American consular officers can't investigate or provide legal representation, but they can express to the host country that the U.S. government is interested in the expeditious and proper handling of the (criminal) case. The consular officers can be the family contact or liaison and provide information on the progress in the criminal case. In Natalee's criminal case with Aruba, the vice-consul was not able to provide information like this. In this regard, I want to try to define some kind of multinational/international cooperation for victims' assistance and develop strategies for cooperation between American and foreign law enforcement agencies in working through these crises.

I can't help but be intrigued by the case of John Mark Karr, arrested in Thailand for confessing to the murder of JonBenét Ramsey. The international cooperation between the authorities in Thailand, the FBI, Homeland Security, International Affairs, and a number of consulates and attachés to extradite Karr shows me that, when there is an American *suspect* in a foreign country, we *can* all work together. But when there is an American *victim* in a foreign country, it's very, very different as far as law enforcement cooperation goes. Isn't there something we can do about that?

Natalee's story is only one of many that need to be told. In Cancun, Mexico, the son of the Alachua County, Florida, sheriff died as a result of falling from a hotel balcony. For five hours the young man lay unconscious until someone called his family to report the accident. It was Father's Day. The sheriff thought the call might be his son wishing him happy Father's Day. The sheriff said he was powerless to get any kind of assistance in Cancun. There was no U.S. State Department representative available. He told me the local authorities were of no help. He described it as a "lawless place." He said there was no police report, no investigation, and no paperwork. He doesn't know what happened to his son, how it happened, or when. No medical procedures were performed on his son in that Cancun hospital. The only paperwork that exists from this sheriff's nightmare is his receipt for the $28,000 he had to pay to get his son's body out of there. He put it on his credit card. If a *sheriff* can't get help from a foreign law enforcement agency, it's easy to see where that leaves the rest of us. The similarities between what the sheriff and I experienced are all too familiar. And they are painful. And they are inexcusable. We need to figure out how to work with other countries to address the needs of our traveling citizens and their families who become victims of crimes or accidents outside this country.

A young woman from the Northeast introduced herself to me after I spoke at the National Organization for Victim Assistance

(NOVA) conference in Orlando, Florida. She was the victim of a very violent crime in the Bahamas. An intruder broke into her room and brutally beat her up, breaking her jaw and other bones in her face. She managed to fight him off and get out of the room, making her way to the front desk of the hotel. The staff there refused to call an ambulance for her, refused to take her to the hospital. She described circumstances very familiar to those in Natalee's case when the hotel staff and "real police" would not respond to the Mountain Brook coach when Natalee disappeared. She stayed in the lobby until her friend discovered her there and summoned help for her. The man who attacked her was identified as one of the hotel bartenders. He was arrested for *breaking and entering*.

It's my opinion that American travelers have a false sense of security. We think all we have to do is call the U.S. embassy and help will be on the way. After all, that's what it implies on the U.S. Bureau of Consular Affairs Web site:

> If you are the victim of a crime overseas contact the nearest U.S. embassy, consulate, or consular agency for assistance.... Consular officers are responsible for assisting U.S. citizens who may be traveling abroad ... and are available for emergency assistance 24 hours a day, seven days a week.

American consulates can also

> help American crime victims with obtaining general information about the local criminal justice process,...

obtain local resources to assist victims,... obtain a list of
attorneys who speak English,...

And they can help obtain things such as police reports.

The U.S. vice-consul assisting us could do very few of these
things. She had no authority, and Aruba knew it. Documents
like police reports, copies of statements, and so forth are critical in filing for victims' assistance compensation. Compensation that's needed, because as we learned, it takes a lot of
money to try to get justice in a crisis like this. We had to live in
Aruba for four months and hire attorneys, investigators, and
searchers as we worked for the answer to what happened to
Natalee. The money spent on professionals, hotel and living
expenses, lawsuit filings, airfares, and more was exorbitant. Victims' compensation and victims' assistance are so important.

Another Bureau of Consular Affairs Web site talks about the
Office of American Citizens Services and Crisis Management.
This is a service to

support the work of overseas embassies and consulates
to provide emergency services to Americans in cases of
death ... crime victimization ... and whereabouts cases.

We sure could have used some of this help in the initial days of
Natalee's disappearance. When tips were coming in. When reports that she had been spotted were numerous and time was of
the essence.

Countries that depend on our tourism dollars need to understand that Americans expect fair treatment and accountability. If

foreign vacation destinations want our money, then they need to be accountable, so that families like the sheriff's, mine, and many others' never have to endure this kind of torture again. They need to know that we want them to take care of us if they expect us to continue to be their source of revenue, their livelihood.

So how do we go about creating a level of cooperation? How do we improve the response time from the U.S. Bureau of Consular Affairs? What can we actually expect from a consular officer when there is a crisis? Is it feasible to look into extradition of foreign suspects who have committed crimes against Americans? Do we need to establish a treaty that would allow the victim's homeland law enforcement officials to participate on their behalf and obtain police reports and other pertinent documents? These are all very difficult and challenging questions. And I don't know the answers or how to get there from here. But Michigan congressman Bart Stupak has invited me to address a law enforcement caucus in Washington, D.C. Perhaps we can propose the Natalee Holloway Travelers' Treaty for law enforcement assistance to American travelers in crisis in a foreign country. And that's a start.

IT'S STILL HARD TO BELIEVE that I've become a tragic expert by necessity and that I'm in a position to share difficult and painful lessons about safety, foreign travel, and personal crisis. But I think the best way I can honor Natalee is to ask these hard questions as well as share information to help people travel more safely, no matter where they go. For instance, activating international calling. Natalee didn't have international calling on her cell phone. That weighs heavily on my heart when I envision her phone sitting there in her luggage, silent. Activating the international calling option is the first thing international travelers should do. I wish I had known before how important this is. What if Natalee could have called one of her friends. Or me? Cingular Wireless was a godsend as we made that first trip to Aruba to find Natalee. All it took was a simple phone call to activate international calling. And it's very inexpensive. Cingular continued to work with our family during our time on the island, and we're very grateful.

Before travelers leave this country they should also activate a temporary medical air-evacuation insurance plan. My son, Matt, recently went to Puerto Rico, but not without coverage by a seven-day medical evacuation plan. This too is comparatively inexpensive when you consider the overall cost of international travel. Had we done this for Natalee, it would have cost about $100. Not the $25,100 it cost for the three days a medical evacuation plane sat idle on a runway in Aruba. No mission or church group, study-abroad group, or travelers of any age should leave the United States without international calling and an evacuation insurance plan.

Travelers should never tell anyone what day they're leaving. Criminals plan to take advantage of travelers when they know it's their day of departure. They know you have to get on a plane, and that you're less likely to call the police to file a report. Natalee disappeared on the last night of her trip. Everyone in Aruba knew it was the Mountain Brook group's last night.

What personal safety boils down to is making a plan. Travelers of all ages must initiate a safety plan to protect themselves, and should start by investigating the destination and learning about the infrastructure there.

I hope that the hotel, travel, and leisure industries will embrace the opportunity to address and study enhanced travel safety. Working with the International Safe Travels Foundation is an opportunity to take travel safety to the next level. No one is asking the industry to guarantee absolutely safe trips. We just need to do all we can to make them *safer*.

For example, the addition of security cameras and the replacement of metal room keys with new high-tech card keys were major advancements in hotel safety. Still, a State Department Web site suggests that international travelers should not rely on their hotel staff for assistance. Why not? Someone should have helped the young woman who was attacked in her room, someone should have helped the sheriff, and someone should have helped the coach from Mountain Brook. Offering assistance does not make the facility accountable for whatever crisis has taken place. Calling for help for a hotel patron who is in trouble is not a black mark, but failing to do so is. Having helpful information available like that which is being compiled by ISTF, so that travelers can quickly access police, attorneys, medical help, and many other resources, is critical. Any hotel, airline, cruise ship, travel agency, or other travel concern that promotes itself as being associated with the ISTF should be more attractive to patrons.

The industry should be able to see the value of getting behind the next phase of the travel-safety movement by supporting the Safe Travels initiative and taking a visible and proactive approach to the subject. Hotel, travel, and leisure customers will appreciate the industries' embracing this idea and endorsing the

International Safe Travels Foundation so that it can grow to serve more travelers.

The foundation is my tribute to Natalee. And I just want this mission to work.

————————

IN THE FIRST SIX MONTHS, the Safe Travels message is delivered in eight states. I think the pinnacle of the spiritual journey is reached when I deliver the message of hope and safety at the Crystal Cathedral in Anaheim, California, where I stand in the pulpit with Dr. Robert Schuller to share my testimony of faith. It's my understanding that the broadcast in which I discuss Safe Travels is heard in more than 120 countries. And the best part about it is that my mother comes to hear me speak for the first time. The good people at the Crystal Cathedral actually let her pick the music for the service. She chooses "Because He Lives" and "How Great Thou Art." It's the most wonderful experience in a long, long time.

In each city I have the privilege to speak to several high schools, churches, or law enforcement and civic groups. This translates to thousands of youths and adults. Delivering this safety message is my triumph over devastation. It gives me great joy and is tremendously rewarding work. I think that I can bear the pain of losing Natalee if it means that I can prevent another family from going through our tragic experience. If even just one young person in tens of thousands is saved, then it's well worth it. I ask young people to make a conscious decision to stay safe. They have to make the choice. And I'm not asking them to do anything more than I ask myself. I have to make difficult choices every day. I have to make a conscious decision every morning when I wake up not to be bitter, not to live in resentment and let anger control me. It's not easy. I ask God to help me. And I know it's not easy for young people to think about choosing not to get into a situation in which they can't defend themselves. But we all have to make hard choices. Every day.

In Natalee's Room

So many outrageous things have happened in the past couple of years that to try to explain them all would consume a thousand pages. It would be *Gone with the Aruban Wind*. And I know this account probably raises as many questions as it answers, and sounds more like a novel than a true story. But it all really happened. To my daughter. To my family. And to me. That's why I'm glad others have been present all along this journey to witness the events. Because they were so incredibly bizarre.

In the end we do finally receive vindication that we have been on the right track all along. After I travel to Holland in 2006 to appear on the popular local *Robert Jensen Show*, the highly respected Dutch investigative reporter Peter de Vries takes an interest an Natalee's case and calls me. His TV crime show in Holland is the equivalent of *America's Most Wanted*. Peter and his team discover and broadcast startling revelations from their own investigation into Natalee's case that we had not heard before. In a television special that airs in Holland, they report findings that absolutely justify the suspicions we have had all along.

First, they discover that a secret meeting took place between Joran's lawyer and the prosecutor in which the lawyer told her that he knows his client played a major role in Natalee's disappearance. Joran's lawyer told the prosecutor this to "clear his conscience," but also told her it was up to her and the police to "get the full proof for this." Next, Peter de Vries reports that Joran almost confessed on June 18, 2005, when a detective called him a "devil." The report says that Joran "lost it" and stated: "I know what you guys think. You think I had sex with Natalee, and that I called my father, and that my father came, and that we hid the body." Peter de Vries reports that he is very suspicious of this statement because the role of Joran's father, Paulus, had not yet been discussed. Further, the TV report states that Joran said out of the blue, "I don't know where she is buried." Again, this subject had not yet been introduced.

The most damning conclusive evidence discovered by this investigative team concerns the search warrant issued for the van der Sloot residence following Joran's arrest. We have always been very distressed that the police could not get into the van der Sloot house in a timely manner. When a search warrant was finally issued ten days after Natalee disappeared, the island police were prepared to go into the home. But according to this report by Peter de Vries, they arrived only to be greeted at the door by a high-ranking official of the prosecutor's office named Ben King, a personal friend of the van der Sloots. So there was no element of surprise. The van der Sloots were more than ready for the police to come. In addition, we learn that the warrant carried by the police did indeed call for the entire premises to be searched, including the house, the gardens, and all the buildings of the property. But it was reduced on the spot by another high-ranking employee of the justice office. Judge commissioner Bob Wit reportedly changed the warrant so that only Joran's apartment could be searched. Peter de Vries said that this was extremely frustrating to the Aruban police, because they had clues that something might have happened to Natalee in the main house or garden area. But they couldn't search there.

The Peter de Vries report concludes that the Aruban police believe that the three suspects never took Natalee to the beach. They believe she met her fate at the van der Sloot home, and that Joran called his father—or someone—and that they disposed of her body. That's what we think may have happened. And there's nothing the police or anyone can do about it, because evil was always two steps ahead. It beat us to the search warrant, and it appeared before we did in the headmaster's office at the International School to explain what happened between Joran and Natalee, and that hotel security cameras weren't working. I knew from the moment I gave my statement at the Bubali police station and saw that torn document with Joran van der Sloot's name on it that we were up against way more than we bargained for. We never stood a chance to get justice for Natalee.

———

DOZENS OF VIDEOTAPES amounting to hours and hours of news interviews people have saved for me lie among the things in the dining room. I don't even recognize that desperate woman on the screen trying to get help for her daughter. Eleven suspects so far have been detained by Aruban authorities and questioned about their connections to one another and the roles they may have played in Natalee's disappearance. These "arrests" cause an occasional resurgence in media interest.

After more than two years of being battered by the tabloids, articles about Natalee still appear in these papers. What makes me as sick as the anguish and suffering I have endured over these articles is the realization that these magazines and their outrageous stories about Natalee appear all over the world. I even saw them in stores in Aruba. Well-meaning individuals who want to express their concerns about these articles send me the tabloids. But this means that even my home is invaded with these distressing and outlandish materials. Even in my dining room—my sanctuary—I can't escape them. And to think that millions and millions of readers worldwide actually believe these stories is more than I can bear. Headlines such as "Natalee's Grave Found," "The Knife that Killed Natalee Plus the Cage Where She was Stashed," and "Natalee's Body Found," to name a few, make me want to vomit. Seeing the growing stack of tabloids also makes me realize that after all this time the articles are becoming even more and more outrageous. And the more bizarre the tabloid stories are, the more freakish I feel. Seeing the headline "World's Biggest Mystery Solved! Natalee Buried Under Cement" takes me right back to the carnival days of the 1960s and makes me feel very, very abnormal. Like a freak in a sideshow. There seems to be no end to this attack, and the emotional distress felt by my son and me is irreparable.

Discussions about what happened to Natalee still abound. Reports of "gypsy boats" that move freely in and out of Aruba to and from nearby Curaçao and Venezuela, and theories of sex slavery, have appeared sporadically in articles. Natalee's name is often mentioned in stories like these.

The idea that Natalee was cremated in Aruba surfaces occasionally. The attorney Vinda told us there is no crematorium there. But many other island residents have told us there is. I was told just a week or two after Natalee disappeared about the murder of the island man who supposedly was the incinerator operator at the oil refinery and also worked part time at the hospital incinerator. He was beheaded by what locals call a "Columbian necktie" and dumped in a cemetery.

The theory that Natalee is at the bottom of the ocean in a fish trap has been a popular hypothesis since fishermen supposedly reported a stolen trap around the time she went missing.

Then there are the bloggers against Natalee and her family who continue to dream up all kinds of bizarre scenarios, like suggesting that she secretly left the island on that medical evacuation plane that was in Aruba for three days when we thought she was going to be brought out of a crack house. Destructive remarks about my daughter are very hurtful. And the people who are making them on the anti-Natalee Web sites generally don't have the guts to sign their names. They hide behind nicknames and made-up locations.

During the writing of this book, the reported two-year deadline of June 9, 2007, came and went during which the Kalpoes and Joran van der Sloot were to be either charged or exonerated as suspects. Around this time media interest again surged as Dutch investigators swarmed the homes of the accused. Then interest fell back. And still there are no answers.

American searchers are still preparing to go back to Aruba to do what they can. They are dedicated individuals who, like so many of us, just still can't comprehend the injustice.

As each Mother's Day, spring break, and anniversary marking Natalee's disappearance draw near, reporters and producers whose names and voices are still as familiar as family call to check in. Even Kathleen, the wonderful FBI victim assistance specialist, still calls. They ask how Matt and I are doing. The media occasionally ask for an interview, and want to know if I've heard anything from Aruba. The answer is always the same. It's my prayer that the unprecedented media attention heaped on our tragedy will somehow have a positive impact on coverage of other missing-person cases. And there are plenty of those. The FBI tells me there are other Natalees around the world, crime victims who were on mission projects or in the Peace Corps, for instance. We rarely hear about those.

Political and law enforcement officials in the United States tell me that we did everything right by getting to the island so quickly, using the media to our advantage, and keeping the political pressure on Aruba as long as we could. Their approval of the way we tried to manage our crisis is very comforting.

———

THE FIRST TIME I DREAM about Natalee is about a year after her disappearance. And it's so good to see her. She's just like she always was, just like I remember her. But the rest of us in the dream are different. And we question each other behind her back about whether she knows she has been gone. Natalee apparently is unaware, and wants to know where her things are. I'm so thankful I can produce what she is asking for, having saved it for her. In my dream she never knows she hasn't been here all along. And the rest of us don't tell her.

The opportunity to expand the speaking engagements continues as the months pass. And I look forward to going to new places and meeting new people, always returning with fresh ideas to make the message better. Natalee is behind me in this mission. I feel it. And I know for sure that Matt is too. But it requires a lot of travel. Twenty states so far, and I intend to visit all fifty. The schedule is demanding. And there is a pull developing between Jug and me. Who could ignore this huge unresolved problem in our marriage—the loss of Natalee—that is now the center of our relationship.

Jug has supported me through this entire nightmare. And we have done everything we can. But how could anyone who knows our saga possibly be surprised when we divorce. We aren't the same anymore. However, Natalee can't take all the blame for the failure of this marriage. We had problems before, but we can't overcome this one.

Rehashing all that has happened doesn't matter anymore. All the suspects who paraded through the revolving door at the police stations, the lost evidence, the witnesses who appeared and dissipated, the lies, the corruption. The whole sketchy ordeal. I know what happened. When Natalee was least able to defend herself, she was taken. Period. Nothing will change the reality that Natalee is gone. And the time has come for me to pack up her things one last time.

Macy the dog comes into Natalee's room and finds me on the floor here as the final good-bye cry comes to an end. She gives me a kiss and wants me to get up off the rug. Get on with what I have to do. Slowly I rise, look around, and begin the heartbreaking task. Carefully I remove Natalee's beautiful white graduation robe from the closet door and fold it up. Next, her petite sundresses with the tags still on them. Pictures of her friends are removed from the bulletin board and distributed among them. And so is her jewelry. It's nice that they all have something special from her. As the packing continues, I try to decide what she would want me to keep and what she would let go. And it's hard. Very hard.

At the top of her closet are some boxes, heavy ones. I pull them down and open them to find Natalee's composition notebook, which is actually a journal from a high-school English class. It's in her handwriting. I have never seen this before. As I open it, I instantly feel her with me right now at this moment, like a physical presence. Overwhelmed with this warmth, I take the journal out and sit down on her bed to read what she has written about love and life.

Jesus Christ is the basis of Christianity and is the most influential person in my life. I believe without him people would be nothing and have no direction in life.

Love is an emotion that happens naturally when one person feels very strongly for another. I believe love is controlled by faith and that certain people are made to love each other. Love is a very complicated emotion. I think I will know when I will find love, because it will be with someone that I care for and cannot live without.

Family is like a deck of cards. You never know what kind of card you'll draw. No one is able to choose their family, but has to accept their own family. I consider myself lucky because I am really happy with the family that I have. To me, family is very important and should be a person's top priority.

I am so taken with the depth of her words, her thoughts. And so relieved that her faith was solid. Just as her Bible group leader said, "Natalee knows how to call on God." Faith has always been a very important part of our lives.

As I read on in the journal, I discover that one of the most moving entries is her description of a hero. Natalee writes:

A hero is someone who puts others before himself. He or she is very selfless and cares about the well-being of others. Heroes also accept life's challenges and remain strong through tough times. They also have a strong sense of determination and stick to goals and morals. I believe that heroes uphold morals and try to encourage others to live life morally correct. Heroes are not only just people called in times of physical danger, but individuals that can both emotionally and physically help people get through rough times. A hero should always show respect for other people as well as respect for himself.

Instantly I realize that Natalee is poignantly describing the people who have reached out to help her family get through this "tough time." It's almost as if she is thanking everyone herself by recognizing the importance of selfless people. And I am amazed at her profound words here. I sit and read the entire journal. Natalee writes about her plans for college and her future, her hopes and dreams, her life. It's a beautiful and wonderful experience through which I manage to complete the depressing task of packing up her room.

———

AS MATT AND I SETTLE into our new home, Natalee's friends come over to help me set up a few of her things in the small area off my bedroom. The *Wizard of Oz* set she never got to see takes its place in the purple curio cabinet. It's comforting to have these things close by and be able to look at these memories that represent Natalee. Who she was. What she did. In her short time here.

I can't say for sure if we'll ever know the answer to whether my daughter is alive or not. I know it doesn't look good. But just as that old metal spiral staircase rose from the ashes when our lake house burned down, so too faith stands strong in the remains of this devastating loss. And just as my dad built another house around that staircase, I will build another life around hope and faith. It won't ever be the same. But I pray that it will, at the very least, be useful.

The hope that filled Natalee's heart fills mine, and I will press on. Faith got me up this morning, and faith will see me through tomorrow. And the next day. And the next. I love Natalee and miss her very much. And still fantasize about the possibility that one day a call will come telling me that I need to go to the island. To get her. I want to always be prepared for that imaginary call. So I keep my passport with me at all times. And right next to mine is Natalee's.

Just in case.

Epilogue

This is a call to action to all the Holiday Inns, Marriotts, Wyndhams, Hiltons, and all other hotel conglomerates; AT&T and other wireless corporations; American Express and other credit card companies; U.S. Airways, Delta, and other airlines; insurance corporations and medical evacuation companies; cruise lines, travel agencies, and all travel-related industries of the world to support the International Safe Travels Foundation. Attendance Marketing, Inc., in Canada and IMN Solutions in Arlington, Virginia, have given generously of their time and resources to get ISTF and the www.safetravelsfoundation.org Web site off the ground. Now it's time to take ISTF to the next phase.

The officers of ISTF receive no salary, and I don't stand to gain anything financially from this invitation. I just want this mission to work. Funding is needed to further the Safe Travels university study and continue to grow the Web site. The travel, hotel, and leisure industries need to embrace the work of ISTF and make information being gathered available for their clients, whether it's at the trip-planning stage with a travel agent or at the front desk of a hotel.

I envision the Web site one day offering important travel data in many languages, so that travelers around the world can log on and get the information they need in their own language. There is much work to be done in travel safety. And the time to get started is now.

Dreams
by Natalee Holloway

Dreams come to us almost every night,
But some are filled with terror and fright,
While others can be of a beautiful sight.

Princesses, castles, horses, and kings,
Prince Charming giving you a lovely ring.
These are all of the fantasy things.

Death, sorrow, heartbreak, and grief,
A tree losing its very last leaf.
These dreams leave us in disbelief.

Some dreams we may always want to keep,
Those that leave us as safe as guarded sheep.
And sadly others may make us weep.

Whatever happens we must always know
Dreams will constantly come and go.
So, always be ready for the next oncoming show.